GET MORE MARCO

IT'S AS SIMPLE AS THIS

1 go.marco-polo.com/phu

2 download and discover

GO!

WORKS OFFLINE!

SYMBOLS

INSIDER TIP   Insider Tip

★   Highlight

● ● ● ●   Best of...

🕊   Scenic view

🌐   Responsible travel: fair trade principles and the environment respected

PRICE CATEGORIES HOTELS

Expensive	over 2715 baht
Moderate	1550–2715 baht
Budget	under 1550 baht

Prices are for two people in a double room or for a bunga-low in a beach resort

PRICE CATEGORIES RESTAURANTS

Expensive	over 385 baht
Moderate	195–385 baht
Budget	under 195 baht

Prices are for a two-course meal without drinks

On the cover: Ko Similan, hot spot for divers p. 79 | Night life on Kata Beach p. 43

MAPS IN THE GUIDEBOOK
(116 A1) Page numbers and coordinates refer to the road atlas
(0) Site/address located off the map.
Coordinates are also given for places that are not marked on the road atlas
(U A1) Coordinates for the map of Phuket Town
Karon, Kata Noi Beach, Kata Yai Beach → p. 41
Patong → p. 51

(🛏 A–B 2–3) refers to the removable pull-out map
(🛏 a–b 2–3) refers to the additional maps on the pull-out map

INSIDE FRONT COVER:
The best Highlights

INSIDE BACK COVER:
Map of Phuket Town

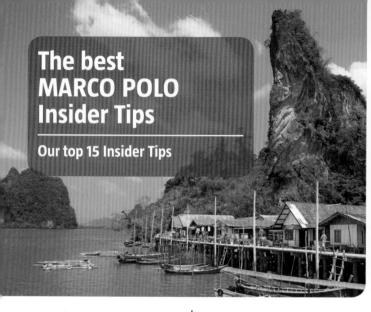

The best MARCO POLO Insider Tips

Our top 15 Insider Tips

INSIDER TIP Yoga on a beach to dream of
Om... – in the exclusive *Renaissance Phuket Resort & Spa* on Mai Khao Beach you can relax completely during yoga sessions on the island's longest beach → p. 46

INSIDER TIP A balcony above the sea
Everyone knows Cape Promthep on Phuket. But there is also a *lookout spot* high above the bay of Nai Harn, where you don't have to share your dream view of the sea with crowds of tourists → p. 64

INSIDER TIP Monkey fun
It's like snorkelling in a gigantic crystal clear fish tank at the dazzling sandy-white *Monkey Beach*. But the beach isn't named after monkeys for nothing so don't leave anything lying around → p. 77

INSIDER TIP Down to the bone
Using a warmed hollow bamboo cane, the treatment at the *De Surin Health Spa* on Surin Beach gives a deeper, firmer and ultimately relaxing massage experience → p. 57

INSIDER TIP Fall in love with this place
Faye's Restaurant on Ko Yao Noi is a pretty café where you can fall in love with the whole unspoiled island while enjoying your vegetarian meal, coffee or cocktails → p. 80

INSIDER TIP Fine dining in a historic location
Enjoy authentic Thai cooking in a beautifully restored town house in the Sino-Portuguese style at the *China Inn* in Phuket Town (photo right) → p. 69

INSIDER TIP Putting in the dark
Golf beneath floodlights? Why not? On *Phunaka Golf Course* near Chalong you can practise teeing off at night → p. 98

INSIDER TIP Shop local
Nestled between beer bars and discounter stores is *OTOP Shopping Paradise* which sells great handmade products made in Southern Thailand → p. 52

BEST OF...

FOR FREE

● *A walk through the swamp*
In Sirinat National Park you can walk through a *mangrove jungle* while keeping your feet dry. The boardwalks allow you to discover a fascinating ecosystem. And there is no admission fee for this part of the national park → p. 45

● *Panorama postcard from the summit*
Get a breathtaking view without feeling shattered: climb the 348 steep steps to the *viewpoint* and watch the twin bays of Ko Phi Phi shimmering beneath you and massive cliffs with green tops rising from the sea... → p. 76

● *A visit to the Chinese gods*
Many residents of Phuket have Chinese ancestors and still worship the gods of those ancestors. You can pay your respects to them in the colourful *Jui Tui Temple* in Phuket Town: from Tean Hu Huan Soy, the god associated with artists, to Kiu Wong (photo) the vegetarian god → p. 66

● *History in a hotel lobby*
A free trip back in time: in the lobby of the *Thavorn Hotel* you can check in, but also see how things looked in Phuket Town before the tourists came. Old photos show views of the town from the days when rickshaw drivers would pedal around here → p. 70

● *Majestic tower*
The *lighthouse on* Cape Promthep was built in honour of the king. Not only does it command a fantastic view of the south coast of Phuket, inside you can admire sextants and marine charts free of charge → p. 64

● *Buried Buddha*
This Enlightened One is definitely worth seeing: the *Golden Buddha* in Wat Phra Thong is firmly planted in the ground – only the upper part of his body is visible. According to a legend, anyone who tries to dig out the statue will die. This attraction costs nothing → p. 37

◖◗◗◗◗● Dots in guidebook refer to "Best of..." tips

Colonial atmosphere

Thailand has never been a colony, yet in *Old Phuket Town* you can definitely sense a colonial atmosphere. A stroll through this old quarter reveals many historic buildings in the Sino-Portuguese style. In *Soi Rommani* you will find one little gem after another → p. 67

Ride the waves

A trip across the waves from beach to beach or to an offshore island is an essential part of a holiday in Phuket. On *Rawai Beach* a whole armada of longtails awaits customers → p. 20, 64

Breach the peace

Buddhist monasteries are generally tranquil places in Thailand. In *Wat Chalong*, however, noise is part of the experience. Visitors set off chains of fireworks – to express gratitude for wishes fulfilled. You too can make a bang in the monastery, as the fireworks are sold on site → p. 59

Sail in the Andaman Sea

The *Andaman Sea* is Asia's number one sailing region, and nowhere will you see more yachts at anchor than off Phuket. Go on board! On the noticeboards of restaurants and bars in the bays of Ao Sane and Chalong, and on Nai Harn Beach, sailors post offers of trips on their private boats → p. 98

Bar hopping

The centre of nightlife in Phuket is *Bangla Road* on Patong Beach. Hundreds of bars are lined up one next to the other, most of them no more than a counter with a roof above it. No other place in Thailand presents such a lively, uninhibited scene at night, with a carnival atmosphere wherever you look. And don't worry, women tourists too are welcome everywhere → p. 53

It doesn't hurt a bit

They stick spikes and hooks into their bodies and feel no pain. Pilgrims at the *Vegetarian Festival* in Phuket Town have entered a trance. Visitors from the West can't exclude the possibility that it might hurt just to look (photo) → p. 104

ONLY ON

BEST OF ...

● **History lessons**
The history of Phuket was shaped by Chinese immigrants. When it's raining, why not head for the *Thaihua Museum*, a converted Chinese school, to find out where they came from and how they lived → **p. 68**

● **Learn to cook Thai**
Rock around the wok! In *Pum's Cooking School* on Patong Beach you can learn what makes the curry creamy and where the spice in prawn soup comes from → **p. 52**

● **Shop until you drop**
You can pass a whole rainy day in *Jungceylon* with ease. Phuket's biggest shopping centre with over 300 shops and a department store can entice even the anti-shopping brigade to join in a spree. And if you get hungry, refreshments are on offer at lots of restaurants (photo) → **p. 52**

● **Below ground**
It never rains here! The *Phuket Tin Mining Museum* is a reconstruction of working life underground, including life-size miners → **p. 73**

● **Fun for the whole family**
A day out at the *Trickeye Museum* stimulates creativity. To get the most out of your visit, come as a family or group where you can have great fun posing in front of three-dimensional paintings and become part of the masterpiece. Don't forget your camera and plenty of time → **p. 68**

● **Meet the sharks**
There's no need to be afraid when you go eyeball to eyeball with the sharks. The glass tunnel through the *Phuket Aquarium* was built to be strong. You can also get close up to swarms of little coral fish → **p. 61**

RAIN

RELAX AND CHILL OUT
Take it easy and spoil yourself

● *Land of milk and honey*
Immerse yourself in the elegant world of the spa at the *Marriott's Mai Khao Beach,* bathing in milk and honey or an arrangement of sweet-scented flowers (photo). For two, it's twice as much fun. Couples can relax together with a romantic spa package → **p. 46**

● *Happy hour on the bay*
A mojito is always a good sundowner. Especially when you have a stunning view to go with it, from the *Reflections Bar* at the *Hotel The Nai Harn* for example, high above the bay of Nai Harn. During Happy Hour you get two drinks for the price of one → **p. 63**

● *(Almost) alone on the beach*
Yes, there are still beaches on Phuket where you can almost count the number of people on the fingers of one hand. Not many tourists find their way to the overgrown bay of *Hin Kruai*. You won't find more Robinson Crusoe feeling anywhere else on the island → **p. 47**

● *Fine dining and sunset experience*
Enjoy the finest global cuisine or a perfectly mixed cocktail at *Joe's Downstairs* while taking in the views over Patong bay. Simply sit back and watch the sun go down against this spectacular backdrop → **p. 51**

● *Give your soul a holiday*
Simply close your eyes and let your thoughts run free like clouds in the sky. *Island Yoga* on Ko Yao Noi provides relaxation for body and soul with meditation and yoga → **p. 81**

● *Luxury on the beach*
Snow-white Kata Beach is wonderful just as it is. But why not add a bit of luxury? If that's what you like, the *Re Ka Ta Beachclub* is the right place. Comfortable sun loungers, light cuisine, many kinds of coffee – hot or iced. And if the sea is too salty for you, you can swim in the pool → **p. 43**

INTRODUCTION

DISCOVER PHUKET!

Stunning beaches and jungle, colourful markets and gigantic shopping temples, a dizzy nightlife and an island capital where the old quarter is being transformed into a lively open-air museum – no wonder Phuket is such a popular holiday destination. The whole world comes here. The island draws more than five million tourists each year. The super-rich anchor their luxury yachts, and regular holidaymakers too relax on Phuket, having a good time and learning from the Thais that life is nicer when lived *with a smile*.

Saffron-coloured monks' robes glow in the light of the morning sun. In elaborately decorated temples, the faithful kneel in front of *Buddha statues that gleam in gold*, holding lotus flowers in their cupped hands. Fishermen tie brightly coloured cloths to the prow of their boats, and taxi drivers hang scented wreaths of jasmine and orchids from the rear-view mirrors of their chugging *tuk tuks*, four-wheeled mini taxis. All of this is intended to attract good fortune and ward off evil, whether on sea or land. Rubber trees stand in straight rows on extensive plantations, *coconut palms* cast feathery shadows on the snow-white and golden-yellow beaches. In little bays, *corals* grow almost up to the shore of fine-grained sand. The sea stretches away to

Playful lightness: a reclining Buddha at the Wat Sirey temple near Phuket Town

the horizon like a carpet of cornflower blue. When you dive in, it's like swimming in a gigantic aquarium. You can almost reach out and stroke fish that are as colourful as confetti. All the *bright shades of the tropics*! Above and below water, this island is a feast for the eyes.

> **Swarms of fish sprinkled like confetti are close enough to touch**

Phuket is *Thailand's biggest island*: 48 km/30 miles long, 22 km/14 miles wide. With a total surface area of 543 km²/209 sq miles (by way of comparison: the city state of Singapore has an area of 640 km²/247 sq miles), it is also the second-smallest of the kingdom's 76 provinces. In terms of its economy, the country's most important holiday destination has a leading position. Only in Bangkok, the capital city and industrial centre of Thailand, 860 km/535 miles away, is the average level of earnings higher than on Phuket. By Thai standards, many of the

1518
The Portuguese found the first trading post for tin

1681
King Narai appoints French missionary René Charbonneau to be governor of Phuket

1785
Burmese invaders besiege Thalang, then the capital city. Thai women dress as soldiers and the Burmese retreat, believing they are outnumbered

1809–1812
Burmese forces land on Phuket three times, burn down Thalang and massacre the inhabitants

340,000 inhabitants are *quite affluent.* They no longer live in wooden houses on piles but in dwellings made of bricks and mortar. They go to work on a motorbike or in their own car. However, it was not international tourism that first triggered a construction boom on Phuket and filled the streets with motorbikes. In Thailand, this island of tin miners, *fishermen and rubber planters* was always regarded as a rich place, even before the first backpackers came from far-away Europe in the 1970s and stayed in huts made of palm fronds on lonely beaches.

The first rubber trees were planted on Phuket in 1903, but even before this an activity that earned many millions had changed the face of the island: *tin mining*. The spread of industrialisation in Europe in the 19th century caused a rapid increase in the demand for tin. Thousands of Chinese labourers came from Malaysia to Phuket to work in the mines. Today about a quarter of the population is of Chinese origin. As late as 1977 the island earned twice as much from tin as from tourism. The decline in extraction began only with a fall in the price of tin in the 1980s.

The ancestors of the Muslim fishermen, too, once came from Malaysia as day labourers. Along with the Chinese and the ethnic Thais, who immigrated from southern China to what is now Thailand about a thousand years ago, they are proud *Khon Phuket*, citizens of Phuket, who all get along together peacefully. Only one small group continues to lead a marginal existence: the *Chao Leh* (literally: sea people, also known as sea gypsies). They are among the first people who settled on the shores of Phuket, but their origins are an enigma to ethnographers to this day. This history of a *multicultural society* is also evident in the places of worship on Phuket. Muslim Thais pray facing Mecca in a whitewashed mosque. Buddhist Thais put their

1897	1903	1906	1950	1976	1980–1990	2001
The first school is opened	The first rubber-tree saplings are planted	EFirst floating tin-extraction platform off Phuket	First bridge to the mainland	Opening of the international airport	Building boom on Patong Beach	Construction work on the last untouched beach

hands together in prayer in a *wat*, a *brightly coloured temple* with an almost playful lightness of character. No less colourful, and adorned with dragons' heads too, are the Chinese temples *(sanjao)*, under whose red roofs both Buddhist and Taoist ceremonies are held.

In *Phuket Town,* several magnificent residences in the Sino-Portuguese style of architecture with artistically designed balustrades and columns, *stucco façades* and round-headed windows serve as reminders of the wealth held by tin and rubber magnates in days gone by. With 70,000 residents, Phuket Town is the administrative and historic centre of the island. However, some tourists don't make it into town even if their holiday lasts several weeks – because they simply don't want to leave the beaches.

There are of course other islands in Southeast Asia for holidaymakers to lie in warm sand, but nowhere else do they find some twenty beaches of high quality, as on Phuket. And what is a *dream beach* for one person might be someone else's nightmare. However, this is part of the charm of Phuket: it has beaches for peace and quiet,

> **Phuket has bustling beaches – and quiet ones too**

or for lots of noise and action. Those who are so inclined can lie down with crowds of others on Patong Beach, and dance the night away to disco music in 1001 bars. Or, for example at the south end of Bang Tao Beach, they can watch fishermen pulling *the day's catch* out of their little boats. Here, the music at night is played by cicadas, and the nightlife is mainly confined to gazing at stars in the sky. Since 2015, though, chairs and loungers are only allowed in small areas on Phuket's beaches (if at all); smoking is forbidden

Phuket is a real pearl, one of the most attractive holiday destinations in Southeast Asia. All traces of the tsunami in 2004 were removed long ago. The same applies to other holiday destinations in southern Thailand. Ferries plough through the waves on the 90-minute trip to the two islands of *Phi Phi*, two tiny sisters that possess a dramatic natural beauty. Tall as skyscrapers, *lime stone rocks* rise vertically above beaches of white sand to be reflected in clear water. This stunning scenery attracts

2004
The tsunami causes the deaths of 5395 people, including 2436 foreign tourists, in southern Thailand. 250 people die on Phuket

2007
The number of visitors to Phuket reaches the five-million mark for the first time

2010
Major investments in Phuket's infrastructure: the government makes 340 million euros available for roads, expanding the airport and the exhibition centre

2016
King Bhumibol Adulyadej dies. His son Maha Vajiralongkorn is crowned as his successor in October

Beach volleyball on Ko Phi Phi: falling over on sand as fine as icing sugar presents no problem really

crowds of visitors. Since Leonardo DiCaprio came here for the filming of The Beach, Ko Phi Phi has become a *party island.* Tourist advertising likes to describe it as one of the ten most beautiful islands in the world. When you push your way through the masses of visitors in the cramped village on the island, you may have your doubts about this, but outside the main settlement there are quiet spots on Phi Phi where you can enjoy the natural splendour in peace – above and below the water, as the island and the islets around it are a *paradise for divers*.

For an truly quiet holiday, head for another pair of sister islands lying even closer to Phuket: Ko Yao Noi and Ko Yao Yai, both of them green oases in the sea, as they are still largely covered by *jungle*. The locals earn a living mainly from

Ko Yao Noi and Ko Yao Yai are green oases

catching fish and tapping rubber trees, and tourists are few and far between. If you like riding a bike through lush vegetation, doing *yoga* watching hornbill birds or simply hanging out in a *hammock* and feeling at peace, these are the perfect islands. On the Yao Islands you get an impression of how things were on Phuket before visitors from overseas came in droves. Here you are in territory that has *hardly opened up to tourism* – so no bars, loungers on the beach or advertising in several languages.

Phuket and the islands confront you with extremely pleasant choices. Whether you prefer peace or action, a stage show or natural beauty – the *island world of the Anaman Sea* has it all. It is never far to the nearest beach – and visitors are met with a friendly smile.

WHAT'S HOT

1 Night shopping

Night markets The twilight hour is when Thai people choose to do their shopping. Night markets have become the absolute hangout for tourists and locals alike. They are the place to see and be seen to catch up with friends and eat tasty and affordable food. Particular favourites in Phuket Town are the large *Weekend Market (Sat, Sun 4–9pm | Chao Fa Rd),* the smaller *Chillva Market (Sun–Wed 4–10pm, Thu–Sat 4–11pm | 141/2 Yaowarat Rd)* and *Walking Street (photo) (Sun 4–10pm | Thaland Rd).*

2 A surfing offshoot

Stand up paddle boarding The latest water sports craze has now hit Phuket: Instead of lying down, boarders stand up on their surfboards and use a long paddle to propel themselves gently along the coast. SUP is great fun and the perfect way to watch the sunset. Courses and tours are organised by *SSS Phuket (Patak Rd. | Kata Yai Beach | www.sssphuket. com), Saltwater Dreaming (Surin Beach | www.saltwater-dreaming.com)* or *Skyla's Surf & SUP (near the Catch Beach Club | Bang Tao Beach | surf-sup.asia).*

3 Eggs and shells

Animal rights European standards of animal welfare still often seem alien to Thais. But awareness of the issue is increasing! The best proof of this is the *Turtle Foundation (photo)* at the *JW Marriott Phuket Resort (maikhaomari neturtlefoundation.org),* which provides infor-mation and practical help. Turtles' nests are guarded, or taken to the breeding station of the institute for marine biology at *Phuket Aquarium.* Another project at the *Aleenta Resort (Natai | www.aleenta.com)* trains local people as turtle guards.

In with the old

Vintage design Grandma's old crackling radio, retro-style bubble gum machines and tiny black and white TVs are highly sought-after in Phuket: More and more cafes and restaurants are now furnished with memorabilia from a bygone era. And even the most ardent technophiles will admit they look pretty cool. *Rasta Café (daily 11am–1am | 15/1 Phuket Rd. | Phuket Town)* has an impressive collection of antique vacuum tube radios while *Old Phuket Town Café (daily 10am–8pm | Thaland Rd/corner of Yaowarat Rd)* is proof that oldies can still be goodies. The lobby in *Quip Bed & Breakfast (54 Phuket Rd)* is decorated with a stack of old TVs and cult ghetto blasters from the 80s – retro is making a real comeback.

Women Power

Muay Thai A wild battle cry can be heard echoing through the hall when the foot of a young woman hits the sand sack – over and over again. What appears brutal to an outsider is in fact the country's national sport. Thai boxing was once a sport reserved for the toughest of men (pinned as "the world's toughest martial art") but is now attracting more and more women taking part in competitions, wanting to keep fit or even shed a few pounds. Because of the hard physical training involved, this strenuous combat sport has become a favourite among body-conscious men and women. The most popular location to train is in the country's biggest boxing centre, *Tiger Muay Thai (Soi Ta-iad | Ao Chalong | www.tigermuaythai. com)*. The trainers at *Sinbi Muay Thai (100/15 Moo 7 | Soi Sai Yuan | Rawai | www.sinbi-muay thai.com)* are all highly skilled in Thai boxing, some even have international success under their belts.

IN A NUTSHELL

LONGTAIL

A ● longtail is not some kind of monkey, but an open motor boat that can often be seen in coastal waters in southern Thailand. These high-prowed wooden boats get their name (in Thai: *hang yao*) from special outboard motors. The propeller, which looks like the tuft at the end of a long tail, is attached to a shaft about 1.5 m/4.5 ft in length and is lowered into the water behind the boat. Longtails were once only used by fishermen, but now they often take tourists on trips along the coast or to offshore islands. As they make a loud droning noise, it is best to bring some ear plugs or look out for a boat that has a silencer fitted to the engine.

You can charter a longtail boat, but only if you hire the captain too. This makes

sense, as the swivel outboard motors mounted horizontally take some getting used to. You will find a *hang yao* on most tourist beaches on Phuket. A whole armada of them awaits passengers on the beach of Rawai (see p. 65).

MANGROVES

They form coastal jungles and a species-rich ecosystem: mangrove forests act as a nursery for young fish, crabs and prawns. Their roots provide a natural breakwater against the waves and protect the land from erosion. The shallow, muddy east coast provides ideal conditions for the growth of mangroves. They have always been felled here to make charcoal – which has not on the whole damaged the environment. In recent

Photo: Kao Phra Thaeo Nationalpark

Longtails and mangrove swamps, Buddhism and bar girls – Phuket is an island with many faces

times trees have been felled on a much larger scale, to make way for large prawn farms.

However, the importance of intact mangrove forests for the environment has now been understood. The government in Bangkok approved an investment of nearly 6.5 million dollars to build a road on the east coast. In order to give as much protection as possible to a mangrove forest near Phuket Town, this road was built on stilts. You can find information on current projects in Thailand and other countries at *www.mangrovesfor thefuture.org*.

MONKEYS & MORE

Only seven per cent of the area of Phuket is now jungle. The largest area of uninterrupted forest is the *Khao Phra Thaeo National Park* in the northeast of the island. This nature reserve is inhabited by porcupines and dwarf deer, but visitors seldom catch sight of these animals. Gibbons and macaque monkeys, which are also extremely shy, swing

the underwater world around Phuket with its plethora of fascinating sea life. You are (almost) guaranteed an unforgettable encounter with anything from tiny neon-coloured fish to giant, harmless whale sharks.

YOU ARE A FALANG

If you learn just one word while you are in Thailand then it's sure to be *falang* and the term is probably being used to describe you, the pale-skinned foreigner. It is a derogative term used to generalise Western tourists yet its origin is unclear – one possible theory is that it is a malapropism of the word *foreigner*. It could also stem from the French *français* because French people are called *farangset* in Thai.

However, it would be rude to call you *falang* to your face. But don't take offense if you are addressed by your first name in the hotel. This is not some kind of artificial over-familiarity but a completely normal way of addressing people in Thailand. VIP celebrities and even the Prime Minister are called by their first names in public yet with a respectful *khun* in front. By the way, this form of address applies to both sexes.

NO PLASTIC

The biggest asset for a holiday island like Phuket is an intact environment. However, the construction boom caused by tourism has had severe effects on the island's natural environment. The water table is falling, energy consumption is rising, and millions of holiday guests per year create a huge amount of waste. Or to be more precise plastic waste - the modern epidemic which seems to have gripped all of South East Asia.

The enormous consumption of plastic bags is an urgent problem. In supermarkets for example, checkout assistants in-

Colourful mini-temple: a place to make offerings to the spirits

through the boughs of the trees, and sometimes a hornbill bird can be seen circling above the jungle. Cobras and pythons slither through the undergrowth, and not only in the wildlife park. Yet as they see humans as their greatest enemy (and justifiably so), the chances that you will encounter one of these exotic jungle creatures in Phuket is pretty slim. You are better off diving down into

stinctively bag even the smallest purchases. So if you say *mai sai tung* ("no bag, please") at the checkout and pack your shopping into your own rucksack, you'll earn double the respect.

OF HUMANS AND ELEPHANTS

The issue of tourists and elephants in Asia is an extremely controversial one. Whether in Thailand, Vietnam or Cambodia, domesticated elephants are used primarily for commercial purposes and are an extremely lucrative business. The elephants are paraded around the streets for stroking and feeding, used in elephant camps, lend their backs to jungle trekkers and even amuse visitors at shows with their ability to paint. Although ageing jumbos are supposed to be put out to rest, they are in reality slaves to the tourist industry working in cities under poor conditions. It is advisable to stay away from the circus shows which often make the creatures perform cruel tricks. Feeding the elephants is as far as you should go.

However, a reversal in trend is in sight: The first travel operators have taken up the mantle and have removed visits to elephant shows from their itinerary. If you should book a safari tour which includes a visit to the elephants, make sure to take a closer look at their living conditions or contact the relevant animal welfare organisations for more information before you go.

AMULET NECKLACES

Many Buddhist Thais can often be seen wearing shiny golden or steel necklaces jangling around their necks with strange pendants hanging from them: Amulets contain tiny figures made of clay, bronze, gold or wood, protected by a clear plastic film and framed in miniature silver and gold shrines. They represent Buddha or other famous monks and are often heirlooms passed down through the family. Amulets are supposed to protect their wearers from accidents and illnesses, theft and life's other adversities. They are sold in many shops and at special markets. Street traders also display their range of amulets on the pavements. Many temples in Thailand also sell amulets where you can have them blessed by monks to increase their chances of working.

CULTURAL FAUX-PAS

In Thailand, you can easily put your foot into it without even noticing. Thais do not like correcting others if they make a mistake or commit a faux-pas. Blatant inappropriate behaviour is simply shrugged off with the words *falang ba,* in other words the pale-skinned foreigner is crazy. But even the Thais lose their patience once in a while, for example when visitors criticize their Royal Family (insulting the monarchy is a criminal offense) or do not show respect to Buddhist elders and icons.

Visitors to the "Land of Smiles" will for sure encounter annoying situations such as an amazingly slow service or a taxi driver demanding extortionate prices. However if you firmly express your opinion, taking care to stay polite and not to raise your voice, you will not cause loss of face for the other person. Because that would be about the worst thing you could do to a local in front of his peers.

HELLO, SIR

In hundreds of bars along Patong Beach so-called bar girls wait for customers to buy them a drink and take them back to their room for a night or spend the whole holiday with them. Most of the women who work in this way come from the poor northeast of Thailand or were lured here from neighbouring countries under false pretences. As sex workers they hope for earnings that they could never achieve from employment in factories or on the fields, for example. They also wish for a better life by marrying a rich man from the West. Nevertheless they are extremely offended if they are described as prostitutes.

practise their Taoist and Confucian rites and rituals in these places of worship.

In the Thai community, Chinese and Buddhist temples play much more a part of everyday life than Christian churches do in the UK. Although there are no official times of service, worshippers regularly visit the temples. If you're planning a journey, having to take an exam or need an operation, then make sure to visit the wat first to ask for help. wat is

Lighting joss sticks: for the Thais, rituals of sacrifice are part of everyday religious life

WAT AND BAHT

95 percent of Thais are Buddhists, making Thailand one of the most Buddhist countries in the world. Phuket is somewhat different: around a third of the population practise Islam and there are more mosques on the island than wats (Buddhist temples). Painted in bright colours and adorned with dragons, Chinese temples are also visible everywhere, especially in Phuket Town. The descendants of Chinese immigrants

actually the term used for a Buddhist monastery but unlike elsewhere the monk community in Thailand does not live a hermetic existence. Tourists and non-Buddhists can visit a wat at any time. Those looking for advice and need help should bring a small offering with them such as incense sticks and garlands. Some believe cash offerings are even better...

SPIRIT HOUSES

They look like miniature temples, standing on platforms in front of houses, shops, hotels and banks – in fact they can be seen everywhere, because spirits can lurk in any place, and these colourful little temples are intended to give them a home. Belief in spirits *(phii)* is deeply rooted in Thai society, and is older than Buddhism. With offerings such as flowers, a bowl of rice or a glass of water, the Thais try to gain the favour of their invisible neighbours and prevent them from wandering around.

It can never do any harm to greet the spirits. Many Thais put their hands together in a *wai* (see below) when they pass the more conspicuous spirit houses, and if they are driving, they sound the horn of the car. You can hear a great deal of hooting when you drive from Phuket Town to Patong Beach, passing the big spirit house on Patong Hill on the left-hand side.

WAI

Thais greet each other not with a handshake but with a *wai*. This involves putting their hands together in front of the chest, with the finger tips pointing upwards. It looks very elegant, and you might think: I like that – I'll do it too! But beware: *wai* does not always mean the same. The gesture can also express an apology, thanks or a request. And the higher the social status of the one being greeted, the higher you'll have to lift your hands. What is more, the order is also important: First, the younger one greets the older one, the one lower in rank the one above him. If you don't know these rules by heart, you should just stick to a friendly nod. Otherwise, you'll easily make a fool of yourself just because of ignorance.

FOR BOOKWORMS & FILM BUFFS

Very Thai: Everyday Popular Culture – In this witty and entertaining coffee table book (2013) full of photographs, Philip Cornwel-Smith tells readers how Thailand "works". Suddenly you will understand all the things about Thai culture that seemed puzzling at first

Sightseeing – Seven stories by Thai-raised author Rattawut Lapcharoensap (2006) set in contemporary provincial Thailand. The author is a great observer of the life of ordinary thais

The Beach – Action-packed film shown on many screens in restaurants and hotels about a young man in search of paradise. Directed by Danny Boyle and starring Leonardo DiCaprio (2000), it was filmed at Maya Bay on the island Ko Phi Phi which has become a magnet for tourists

Tsunami: The Aftermath – television mini-series that was broadcast in two parts in 2006. It dramatizes the events following the 2004 tsunami in Indonesia and its neighbouring countries, including Thailand. Starring Tim Roth and Toni Collette, it was filmed in Phuket and Khao Lak, Thailand

FOOD & DRINK

Culinary treats on Phuket are as international as the visitors to the island. Here you can get fish and chips, pizza or paella. But if you are planning a journey of gastronomic discovery, don't fail to try the light, fresh and aromatic cooking of the Thais.

The sounds of steaming and sizzling come from little eateries on every corner. *Mobile food stalls* park by the side of the road, the cook places a few stools and small tables on the pavement, and hey presto! – you have an open-air restaurant serving noodle soup with chicken or duck, fried rice with prawns or sweet pancakes with pineapple for just a few baht.

Thailand's low-fat food is so *healthy* that nutritionists love it. Red meat is used in small quantities, while *poultry and sea food* are eaten more often – with plenty of herbs and spices. Vegetables are cooked briefly so that they stay crisp and keep their vitamins. Thai cuisine is also perfectly adapted to the tropical climate. Meals spiced up with *chilli* provide protection against bacteria and are good for the circulation, which can be affected by the high humidity. The food is light and easy to digest.

Thai dishes are served in bite-sized pieces, and eaten holding a spoon in the right hand. Only dishes with *noodles* – including soup! – are served with chopsticks. A typical Thai menu can consist of courses with up to five different kinds of flavours. Their combination stimulates the taste buds, and is accom-

Photo: Shrimps with rice and hot red sauce

Made in heaven, and as hot as hell –
Thai food is not only light and healthy,
but absolutely delicious

panied by a ***big bowl of rice.*** All the diners help themselves. It is considered impolite to heap up all the items onto your plate at once.

Only higher-class restaurants have fixed times for *lunch* (11.30am–2pm) and dinner (6.30pm–10pm).

On Phuket, as everywhere in the south of Thailand, the taste of neighbouring Malaysia is ever present. One example is ***gaeng massaman,*** a red curry with beef, peanuts and chunks of potato. Inhabitants of an island are extremely keen on sea food, of course. However, the coastal waters have been overfished, and the famous ***Phuket lobster*** (not actually a lobster but a kind of langoustine) usually comes from a fish farm. Its smaller relatives, prawns and shrimps *(gung),* are almost all produced on the farms that have been established along many stretches of the coast and on Phuket itself.

Thais love hot, spicy food. In tourist restaurants the use of chilli is more sparing, but if you are concerned about spicy

LOCAL SPECIALITIES

gaeng kiau wan gai – This green curry with chicken and aubergines is a delicacy to make you sweat. Slightly sweet (*wan*)

gung hom pa – Prawns in batter. You dip them in tartare sauce or in a sweet-sour vinegar with chilli rings (photo left)

kao pat – Fried rice may not be haute cuisine, but it is a filling meal – made with egg (*kai*) and vegetables (*pak*). Other ingredients that can be added are shrimps (*gung*), pork (*mu*) or chicken (*gai*)

kui tiao nam – This noodle soup is Thailand's favourite snack. Food stalls make it on every corner. Usually with pork (*mu*) or chicken, but it tastes particularly good with duck (*pet*)

plamuk tohd katiam pik thai – Pieces of squid fried with garlic and pepper (not hot), always a tasty snack

pla piau wan – This sauce with sweet and sour fried fish is served with a lot of colourful vegetables and pieces of pineapple

som tam – Salad made from thin strips of green papaya with cocktail tomatoes, dried shrimps, small crabs and lots of chilli. Raw vegetables, sticky rice and charcoal-grilled chicken (*gai pat*) go well with it

tom kha gai – This soup of chicken in coconut milk is an exotic treat. Beware: there are entire chilli pods in the spicy liquid

tom yam gung – This sour prawn soup is Thailand's unofficial national dish. It gets its unmistakable taste from lemongrass, and its spiciness from chilli. Always eaten with rice

yam wunsen – Salad of glass noodles with herbs, shrimps and minced pork. Chilli adds heat (photo right)

food, order a dish with the words *mai peht* (not hot). Standards such as fried rice and noodle soup are usually seasoned by the guests themselves, using coarse chilli powder, sugar or a **sweet-and-sour vinegar** in which pieces of fresh chilli float. *Nam pla* (fish sauce) is used instead of salt. When chopped chilli is added, the fish sauce is known as **nam pla.** Take care with the quantity! Side salads in the Western style, for example with lettuce or tomatoes, are not eaten by the Thais. A typical *Thai salad (yam)* is more of a dish in itself and is often eaten between main meals. It is almost always hot, especially the filling *yam nüa*, a salad with a sour taste made from strips of beef garnished with garlic, coriander, onions and powdered chilli. A popular dish known as *yam wunsen* has *glass noodles* as the main ingredient.

Thais love sweet treats – the sweeter the better. Small, home-made, mega-calorie creations in all colours of the rainbow can be bought from stalls at festivities, markets and on the street. One delicious snack that is not extremely sweet is *sticky rice* cooked in coconut milk, which today is still served prettily wrapped in banana leaves. Visitors to Phuket can sample all the *fruit of the tropics.* The locals consider *durian* to be the queen of fruits. It is also known as stinkfruit, for a good reason. The yellowish-white flesh within the prickly outer skin has a creamy softness. Either you can't resist it, or it makes you shudder. By contrast everyone likes a *mango (mamuang)*, which tastes extremely good with concentrated coconut milk and sticky rice *(kao niau)*. The Thais also love strips of green mango, which they dunk in a mixture of sugar and chilli. Beneath the thick, wine-red skin of the *mangosteen (mangkut)* is a white flesh that tastes sweet and a little bit sour at the same time. It is also worth trying a hairy *rambutan (ngo)*, a delicious lychee *(linchi)* or the red Java apple *(jompu)*.

The availability of freshly pressed fruit juice is mostly limited to orange juice – which is often diluted with lemonade. Other thirst-quenchers are water *(nam bau)* and mineral water, as well as a variety of soft drinks. The most popular *local brands of beer* are *Singha* and *Chang*, and international brands such as *Heineken* and *Tiger* are also brewed in Thailand. Imported European beer is sold in many bars.

Thais know that the appearance of a meal is important

A cheap spirit named *mekhong* is distilled from rice, and sometimes described as "whisky". *Saeng som* (made from sugar cane) is more expensive and has a less perfumed flavour, but this one too should not be drunk neat. With soda water and a shot of lime juice it makes an *iced long drink*. Tourists like to mix it with cola.

SHOPPING

Almost everything that is sold on Phuket comes from other parts of the country and is relatively expensive. If you are also visiting Bangkok or Chiang Mai in north Thailand, you should make your purchases there. The best places for shopping on Phuket are the island's capital and Patong Beach. Environmentalists advise you not to buy shells and corals. Shellfish are taken alive out of the sea and boiled to get the shells, while trading in corals is prohibited.

ANTIQUES

Trustworthy shops will draw your attention to the fact that an export permit is required for antiques, and will obtain one for you. If you do it yourself, the procedure can be complicated. Information is available from the National Museum in Thalang *(tel. 076 31 14 26)*.

BUDDHA STATUES

The Thai customs authorities are particularly sensitive if they discover Buddha statues in tourists' luggage. Even the cheapest plastic Buddhas may not be exported without a permit! Only amulets to be worn on the body may be taken out

of the country. You can apply for an export permit at the National Museum in Thalang – so long as it is not for a statue of historic value, which may not be exported at all.

CLOTHING

Every other shop near the beaches seems to be a tailor. Arrange for at least two fitting sessions and be sure to have alterations made if the clothes do not fit. The largest selection of ready-made clothes is available from *Patong Beach*, the *Central Festival* shopping centre and the *Robinson department store* in Phuket Town. In some textile shops in town (e.g. in *Thalang Rd.)* you will find the typical Thai cloth that is called *pa kao ma*. Worn as a short sarong in rural areas, it can also be used as a sash, shawl, head covering or towel. This all-purpose cloth usually comes in a red-and-blue or red-and-white check pattern. It fades when washed frequently, but becomes softer. Batik cloths are also made on Phuket, so you can take all the bright colours of the tropics home with you for a modest price.

Spices, clothes, gold and antiques –
while Phuket is not exactly a shoppers
paradise, you will find souvenirs here

GOLD

Gold jewellery of up to 23 carats is sold
in special gold shops (not at the jewel-
lers!), which can be recognised by their
red interior fittings. Prices depend on the
current price of gold. This high-quality
jewellery can be resold, possibly at a
profit if the price of gold rises. The best
choice of gold jewellery is to be had in
Phuket Town.

JEWELS AND PEARLS

Be extremely careful when buying pre-
cious stones. Don't let touts persuade
you to go into a shop, and never buy
from street traders. Phuket is one of the
leading places for buying pearls. To find
out how to tell the difference between
real and artificial ones, visit a pearl farm
(e.g. on the island of Naka Noi, to which
you can book a trip at a travel agent).

PAINTINGS

A Picasso for about 40 dollars? No problem, you can have one – not an original,
but a masterly copy. In Phuket's tourist
centres a number of local artists have
specialised in copying the work of their
world-famous colleagues. Holidaymakers can have their portrait painted without having to sit for hours – a passport
photo is all you need. Original Thai paintings by Thai artists are sold at the galler-
ies in the old quarter of Phuket Town.

SPICES

Pepper or cinnamon, chilli, curcuma or
curry paste – exotic spices cost only a
fraction of the price you would pay at
home. All the big supermarkets, *Tesco
Lotus* for example, are extremely well
stocked. Prices are lowest at the market
in Phuket Town.

THE WEST COAST

What a coast! Green hills shelter beaches that go on for miles and small bays from the rest of the world. Holidaymakers from all over the globe come here to find peace and quiet – or lots of activity. On the west coast, which measures 50 km/30 miles from north to south, Phuket is at its best. Nature has created top-class beaches here – with a total length of 35 km/22 miles – so this is where you'll find almost all the beach resorts, and where visitors come for the sun. Patong Beach is Phuket's tourist centre, a town by the sea where sun loungers are lined up several rows deep. The further north you go, the quieter things become, and you can still discover beaches and bays where the palms and other trees outnumber the sunshades.

BANG TAO BEACH

(118 A–B 2–3) (*C7*) This 6 km/3.5 mile-long beach, fringed by palm trees and casuarinas, has always been in pristine condition, but until the 1980s its hinterland, ruined by tin mining, looked as barren as the moon. Enter the Laguna Project. The deserted tin mines were flooded and a green landscape of lagoons by the sea with seven high-class resorts was created. Nevertheless, outside this impressive oasis of luxury Bang Tao has remained largely authentic to this day. On the southern part of the beach you will find

Relaxation beneath palm trees or action into the small hours – everything is possible on the quiet bays and long beaches in the west

a small tourist village with shops and cafés. More expensive shops and restaurants are situated on the access road to the Laguna Resort.

At Choeng Thale further inland the life of the mainly Muslim population has hardly been changed at all by tourism. The people still work as fishermen, farmers and traders. For Friday prayers they all assemble at the Islamiya Mosque, the largest mosque on Phuket.

The over 30 restaurants in the seven Laguna Resorts will satisfy even gourmets with high expectations. On the beach in front of the resorts there are a number of open-air restaurants that specialise in seafood. For a romantic evening for two, the *Banyan Tree* on the lagoons organises INSIDER TIP sunset dinner cruises *(Sanya Rak)* in a longtail (book in advance). On Lagoon Road (leading to the Laguna Resorts) a lot of restaurants have

Motorcyclists in front of Phuket's largest mosque, the Islamiya Mosque in Choeng Thale

been established, some of them of excellent quality.

INSIDER TIP ▶ CATCH BEACH CLUB

Trendy club directly on the beach with pool and exclusive atmosphere. The menu is a mixture of Western-style dishes as well as hot and spicy Thai cuisine. The venue plays relaxing lounge music during the daytime while a DJ sets a party vibe evenings with dance music. See for yourself by visiting the website and watching the scenes from the live webcam. *Daily 10am until late | 202/88 Moo 2 | Cherngtalay | tel. 06 53 48 20 17 | catchbeachclub.com | Moderate*

INSIDER TIP ▶ DEDOS

Pablo, who learned to cook from Bocuse, produces top-quality Mediterranean cuisine with Thai and Japanese touches. His breast of duck with sweet and sour tamarind sauce is delicious. Pick-up service. *Daily from 6pm | Lagoon Rd. | tel. 076 32 51 82 | www.dedos-restaurant.com | Expensive*

NOK & JO'S

Rustic style at the southern end of Bang Tao on the road to Surin. Here you can eat goulash as well as a Thai curry and different kinds of bread and wine to go with it. Barbecue all you can eat every Wednesday and Sunday. You can even play table football and pool here. *Daily 10am–1am | tel. 0815 38 2110 | Budget*

INSIDER TIP ▶ TATONKA

The proprietor of this restaurant is widely travelled, which you notice when Pizza Peking Duck meets Sashimi spring rolls on the menu. *Daily from 6pm | 19 Lagoon Rd. | tel. 076 32 43 49 | Moderate*

TOTO RESTAURANT

Roberto's spaghetti vongole, calzone and tiramisu taste just as good as in Italy. *Daily from 3pm | Lagoon Rd. | tel. 076 27 14 30 | www.totophuket.com | Moderate–Expensive*

XANA BEACH CLUB WITH ATTICA

Situated directly at the beach, this stylish restaurant and club restaurant serves international food (seafood barbecue on Fridays) and has a good selection of wines. The club has a 35m long pool and DJs get the party started in the evenings. *Daily 10am–11pm | near Angsana Laguna Resort | tel. 076 32 41 01 | www.xana beachclub.com | Moderate*

SPORTS & ACTIVITIES

The Laguna Resorts offer water sports, tennis, golf and squash. At *Quest Laguna Adventure (tel. 076 32 40 62)* there is a climbing wall that you can tackle with safety equipment. *Dusit Laguna (www. lagunaphuket.com)* hires out bikes and organises cookery courses. At the *Banyan Tree Phuket* you can learn batik painting or relax with meditation and tai chi. The facilities in the resorts are open to all guests of the Laguna complex.

ENTERTAINMENT

Party the night away on the beach in the company of the coolest hipsters either in the *Xana Beach Club* (see above) or further south in *Catch Beach Club* (see p. 34) which attracts a mixed crowd from all over the world after relocating here from Surin Beach.

WHERE TO STAY

ANDAMAN BANG TAO BAY RESORT

A cosy little resort with extremely tasteful cottages right on the beach and a small pool. *16 rooms | 82/9 Bang Tao Beach | tel. 076 27 02 46 | www.andamanbang taobayresort.com | Expensive*

BANGTAO VILLAGE RESORT

Well-kept holiday cottages with lots of greenery and a small pool. All rooms are equipped with air-conditioning, TV and refrigerator. Located in a quiet side street in the town, the resort is about a ten minutes' walk from the beach. *28*

★ **Wat Phra Nang Sang and Wat Phra Thong**
Pretty as a picture: two temples on the highway near Thalang, radiant with colourful murals and lots of gold → p. 37

★ **FantaSea**
Spectacular show with hundreds of performers as a celebration of the imagination → p. 38

★ **Viewpoint**
Three beaches lining the sea like pearls below you – the viewpoint at Kata gives you a fantastic view over the sea and the beach → p. 42

★ **Mom Tri's Kitchen**
A lovely garden restaurant with works of art, a sea view and culinary surprises → p. 43

★ **Trisara**
Luxurious but expensive: Phuket's best resort is a paradise of wood and marble, pools and sea views above a small beach to die for → p. 44

★ **Simon Cabaret**
Gaudy transvestite revue with music, dance and comedy – 50 "ladies" in lavish costumes → p. 54

MARCO POLO HIGHLIGHTS

rooms | Srisoonthorn Rd. | tel. 076 27 04 74 | www.bangtaovillageresort.com | *Expensive*

BANYAN TREE PHUKET

Elegant and exclusive houses, some with their own pool (9 x 13 m/30 x 45 ft) that you can almost dive into from your bed. Excellent spa (no medical staff) with sauna, massage, meditation, yoga, aromatherapy, pool with current. Definitely number one among the Laguna Resorts. *150 rooms | Bang Tao Beach | tel. 076 32 43 74 | www.banyantree.com/en/ap-thailand-phuket-resort | Expensive*

BEST WESTERN PREMIER BANGTAO BEACH RESORT & SPA

The luxurious rooms and villas have a direct, private access to the beach. Two swimming pools, two restaurants and a spa offer the ultimate in relaxation and pleasure. *243 rooms | Choeng Rd. | tel. 076 27 06 80 | www.bangtaobeach.com | Expensive*

DUSIT LAGUNA

Lagoons to the right, lagoons to the left, and in front the sparkling sea. *Dusit* is surrounded by tropical gardens like an island in a sea of green. The architecture and interior fittings were designed with attention to Thai style. *254 rooms | 390 Srisoonthorn Rd. | tel. 076 36 29 99 | www.dusit.com | Expensive*

INFORMATION

Information on the Laguna complex: *Laguna Phuket (tel. 076 36 23 00 | www.lagunaphuket.com)*, on Bang Tao Beach: *www.phuket.com/island/beaches_bang tao.htm*

WHERE TO GO

KHAO PHRA THAEO NATIONAL PARK ⊙ (119 D1–2) (𝄞 E5–7)

Head into the jungle and get back to nature at its wildest. Three off-road hiking routes take you into this national park where you can explore its wild beauty – but make sure you don't head off on your own. Sturdy shoes and mosquito spray are essential and if you prefer to be on the safe side, hire a guide from the national park office. However, the route to the *Ton Sai Waterfall* is easy to find on your own. Don't miss out on the *Gibbon Rehabilitation Centre (daily 9am–4pm | free admission | www.gibbonproject.org)*, where you can get up close to these lovable animals. *National park entrance fee 200 baht | turn-off to the park at the crossroads in Thalang*

THALANG NATIONAL MUSEUM/ HEROINES MONUMENT (119 D3) (𝄞 E7–8)

12 km/7.5 miles east of Bang Tao, road no. 4025 leads to the *Heroines Monument*, which is situated in the middle of the intersection with Highway 402. It commemorates two sisters, Chan and Muk, who saved Phuket from destruction by the Burmese in 1785. They created the impression of a huge army by clothing all the women as soldiers and mobilising them alongside the men.

Beyond the intersection on road no. 4027 on the right, the *Thalang National Museum* offers a small but well-conceived presentation of the history of Phuket. The exhibition includes prehistoric archaeological finds, items of everyday use, crafts and old weapons. *Daily 8.30am–4.30pm | admission 100 baht*

WAT PHRA NANG SANG/WAT PHRA THONG ★

(118 C1) (*D6*)

Two temples situated on Highway 402 in Thalang are worth a visit. The elegant *Wat Phra Nang Sang* (after the crossing with road no. 4030 go right towards Phuket Town, approx. 6 km/4 miles from Bang Tao Beach) is the oldest on the island. It was built about 250 years ago, when Thalang was the capital of Phuket. Colourful murals relate the history of Phuket and the fall of Ayutthaya.

said that anyone who tries to dig out the statue or shows disrespect towards it will die.

KAMALA BEACH

(118 A3–4) (*B–C 8–9*) **Tourism came late to this flat bay. In the village of the same name, which stretches far inland, life continues peacefully as it used to, but this village idyll is attracting more**

Glowing colours: murals in Wat Phra Nang Sang, the oldest temple on Phuket

Wat Phra Thong (just before leaving town turn right towards the airport) is home to a ● Buddha figure covered with a thick layer of gold leaf which is the subject of legends. Only the upper part of the statue is above ground. It is

and more foreigners who come to live on Phuket and build fine houses for themselves here.

Although a full tourist infrastructure exists here, do not expect too much of the shopping and nightlife.

KAMALA BEACH

FOOD & DRINK

Lots of places along Beach Rd. specialise in seafood. *Charoen Seafood (Moderate)*, which belongs to the *Kamala Dreams* resort, always has plenty of customers. In the *Kamala Bakery (Budget)* on the main

Wonderland: FantaSea is a gigantic show complex

road you can order cakes and filled baguettes to go with your cappuccino.

936 COFFEE
Sometimes all you need is a good cup of coffee to start your day off the right way. That's maybe why some customers come back to this coffee shop day after day for its great coffee, tasty breakfast and a

great view of this lively street. *Daily 8.30am–10pm | 3/6 Moo 3 | tel. 08 12 56 70 71 | Budget*

GREEK TAVERN
If you're looking for a change from Thai food, try the souvlaki, tzatziki and other Greek specialities at this taverna. *Daily 10.30am–1opm | 71/20 Moo 3 | Soi Kamala 10 | tel. 09 20 06 39 34 | Moderate*

GRILL BILL
If a tasty steak from the barbecue sounds good, head to the best grill in Phuket which also serves excellent fish dishes, pasta and burgers. *Daily from 10am, off season from 6pm | 86/16 Rim Haad Rd. | tel. 08 13 97 35 79 | Moderate*

KOKOSNUSS
For all fans of German sausages, Thomas from Nuremberg serves the speciality of his home town, as well as fresh bread with cheese and different kinds of cold sausage. A German buffet is served five nights a week. *Daily 7am–11pm | Soi 7 (an alley off Beach Rd.) | tel. 0815 38 52 85 | www.phuketkokosnuss.com | Budget–Moderate*

SHOPPING

In the *Kamala Center & Shopping* at the edge of the village on the Patong road, every day is market day – especially for the locals. The stalls sell more or less everything from flashlights and crockery to cheap clothes. And of course there are Thai snacks to keep you going between meals.

ENTERTAINMENT

FANTASEA ★
A show straight from a fairy tale (unfortunately including trained elephants

and other animals) is presented in an arena for 3000 spectators at the *Fanta-Sea* fun park. The 75-minute show offers a spectacular insight into the Thai culture and history. For 300 baht per person guests are picked up from hotels all over Phuket in minibuses and taken home afterwards. *Admission 1800 baht, with an opulent dinner buffet 2200 baht | tel. 076 38 51 11 | www.phuket-fantasea.com*

WHERE TO STAY

You will find several guesthouses in the stretch between the main road and the beach, including the cosy *Sabina Guesthouse (9 rooms | Kamala Beach | tel. 076 27 95 44 | www.chezsabina-guesthouse. com | Budget)*, run by the helpful Mr Phitsanu. Basic, but with TV, fridge, air conditioning.

INSIDER TIP BAAN CHABA

Pleasant cottages with air conditioning and minibar in an attractive, green little complex. The beach is only a few paces away. *8 rooms | Kamala Beach | tel. 076 27 91 58 | www.baanchaba.com | Moderate*

THE CLUB

On the main road, approx. five minutes from the beach, this resort offers excellent value for money. Pleasant rooms with TV, small kitchen, air conditioning. Small pool. *22 rooms | Main Rd. | tel. 0818 93 49 11 | www.the-club.phuket.ag | Budget–Moderate*

KAMALA BEACH RESORT

The largest resort in Kamala, right on the beach. Extremely comfortable rooms with TV, minibar. Four pools. *414 rooms | Kamala Beach | tel. 076 27 95 80 | www. kamalabeach.com | Expensive*

INSIDER TIP PAPA CRAB

What was once a travellers' hostel has turned into a well-kept boutique resort with stylish rooms for non-smokers. Low-key design and words of wisdom to decorate the walls. Only two minutes from the beach. *10 rooms | Beach Rd. | tel. 076 38 53 15 | www.phuketpapacrab.com | Moderate*

KARON BEACH

MAP ON PAGE 41
(120 A–B 3–4) (*C11–12*) **On this 4 km/2.5-mile-long beach, fringed with bushes and trees, it does not get crowded even in high season.**

Almost all the resorts along with the shops and restaurants are on the other side of the beach road, which does not have heavy traffic. A tourist village has sprung up in the north around the *Karon Centre* next to the roundabout *(Karon Circle)*. Along the beach road some remaining open spaces with palms and undergrowth ensure that Karon often seems almost deserted, even in high season. This is a good choice for those who like things neither too quiet nor too noisy.

FOOD & DRINK

The best-value seafood is served in the basic open-air restaurants at the south end of Karon near the football stadium and at the north end near the roundabout.

OLD SIAM RESTAURANT

Outstanding Thai food served on the terrace, or indoors, where diners sit on the floor to enjoy a *Kanthoke dinner* typical of northern Thailand, with the dishes served on low tables. On Wed and Sun at 8.50pm classical Thai dances are performed. In the *Thavorn Palm Beach Resort. Daily lunch/dinner | 128/10 Karon Rd. | tel. 076 39 60 90 | Moderate–Expensive*

ON THE ROCK

Pleasant open-air restaurant in the *Marina Cottage* resort on the rocky slope by the sea. The seafood and Thai dishes are as good as the view. *Daily lunch/dinner | tel. 0 76 33 06 25 | Moderate–Expensive*

SPORTS & ACTIVITIES

You can hire a surfboard on the beach, go water skiing or parasailing. Also diving schools.

ENTERTAINMENT

Nightlife on Karon Beach is restricted to a few bars in the tourist village at the north end and in the middle of the beach.

Land in sight: Conquering Kata Beach on a longtail boat

WHERE TO STAY

IN ON THE BEACH

The comfortably furnished rooms in this two-storey building are clustered around a pool so it's just a few steps to the water. *46 rooms | 395–397 Moo 1 | Patak Rd. | tel. 076 39 82 20 | www.karon-inonthebeach.com | Moderate*

INSIDER TIP KARON CAFÉ INN

A pleasant guesthouse with good food. TV, refrigerator and air-conditioning in every room. Only 150 m/150 yd to the beach. *16 rooms | Soi Islandia Park Resort | tel. 076 39 62 17 | www.karoncafe.com | Moderate*

MARINA PHUKET RESORT

Jungle-green complex with high-class wooden bungalows on a rocky headland that divides Karon from Kata Beach. Small pool with direct access to the beach. *89 rooms | 47 Karon Rd. | tel. 076 33 06 25 | www.marinaphuket.com | Expensive*

RAMADA PHUKET SOUTHSEA

Comfortable hotel boasting a large pool, with only the road separating it from the beach. *152 rooms | 204 Karon Rd. | near Karon Circle | tel. 076 37 08 88 | www.ramadaphuketsouthsea.com | Expensive*

KATA NOI BEACH

MAP ON PAGE 41

(120 A–B5) (*C13*) **The small *(noi)* Kata Beach is beyond the hill, approx. 15 minutes' walk from the big *(yai)* Kata Beach.**

This bay 1 km/0.5 miles long, with a sandy beach as white as new-fallen

snow, is that little bit more beautiful than its larger neighbour, and is also quieter. Kata Noi is like a natural Roman amphitheatre that opens to the sea, flanked by green hills. The elongated *Kata Thani Phuket Beach Resort* domi-nates the beach but does not rise above the palms and casuarinas, nor block access to the beach. Otherwise there are only a few small hotels, basic restaurants and a handful of shops here.

Spoilt for choice of pools in the Katathani Phuket Beach Resort

WHERE TO STAY

KATA THANI PHUKET BEACH RESORT

Tastefully furnished rooms, five restaurants (with European and even Brazilian food), five pools, tennis courts, a gym as well as a sauna – the Kata Thani leaves no wish unfulfilled. It is also environmentally friendly: wastewater is recycled to keep the gardens green, organic fertilisers are used, kitchen leftovers are converted to biogas and some of the hot water is heated by solar cells. *480 rooms | 14 Kata Noi Rd. | tel. 076 33 0124 | www.katathani.com | Expensive*

WHERE TO GO

VIEWPOINT ★ ☆ (124 B5) (𝄞 C13)

High above the sea, you can enjoy a wide-ranging view of the two Kata beaches and of Karon Beach, with beautiful, radiant white crescents of sand lined up like pearls on a chain. The official name for this spot is *Karon Viewpoint*, as it is in the territory of Karon district, to which Kata and Kata Noi belong. There are places to park on the road, and a few stands sell snacks, drinks and souvenirs. A covered pavilion provides shade. *From Kata Noi back towards Kata, turn right onto road no. 4233 (towards Nai Harn) directly behind the hill, after 2 km/1.25 miles*

KATA YAI BEACH

MAP ON PAGE 41

(120 B4–5) (𝄞 C12–13) **A crescent-shaped bay 2 km/1.25 miles long with a superb beach and pure, clear water.**

Almost three quarters of the bay has been occupied by the Club Med, but via the beach road in front of the club you can reach the sea everywhere. Two holiday villages, one at each end of the beach, supply everything tourists need. From the northern village, however, it takes almost ten minutes to get to either Karon beach on the right or to Kata Yai beach on the left. This is a very crowded place; traffic is heavy in the main season. There are many smaller resorts and guesthouses here, and therefore fewer people on package holidays than on Karon Beach. If you prefer things not to be too quiet, but don't like a place with big hotels, Kata Beach is the right destination.

FOOD & DRINK

THE BOATHOUSE WINE & GRILL
Elegant but casual, with a terrace right on the beach. Both the Thai meals and the international dishes are first class, and the wine list offers an excellent selection. *Daily 7am–11.30pm | in the Boathouse resort | 182 Khok Tanot Rd. | tel. 076 33 05 57 | Expensive*

LA CAPANNINA
If most of the guests in an Italian restaurant are Italians, and if the pizza is reputed to be the best on the island and if the same friendly staff have been serving to the best standards for years then you know the restaurant must be good. *Daily 11am–11.30pm | 98/84-85 Kata Rd. | tel. 08 13 67 49 94 | capannina.co.th | Moderate*

INSIDER TIP KAMPONG KATA HILL
This romantic Thai restaurant built from wood lies high on a hill in the middle of Kata. Steaks are served, but fish with chilli sauce is a better option here. *Daily dinner | Kata Centre | Taina Rd. | tel. 076 33 01 03 | Moderate*

MOM TRI'S KITCHEN ★ ☼
An unusual eatery high above the sea on a promontory between Kata and Kata Noi. A fusion of Asian and Mediterranean cooking. Attached to a high-class resort, the restaurant is adorned with works of art and a culinary highlight. Booking recommended. *Daily lunch/dinner | 3/2 Patak Rd. | tel. 076 33 35 68 | www. momtriphuket.com | Expensive*

RE KA TA BEACHCLUB ●
A pleasant place where you can relax on the beach until late at night, with a pool, spa and loungers, light meals, cocktails and many kinds of coffee. The 1000 baht admission charge is deducted from the cost of food and drink. *Daily 9am–midnight | Koktanode Rd. (near the Boathouse resort) | tel. 076 33 04 42 | Expensive*

SHOPPING

You will find everything for your daily needs here and of course all kinds of souvenirs. Fashionable beachwear is sold at INSIDER TIP *Barü Fashion (Beach Rd. opposite Marina Beach Resort | www.baru fashion.com).*

SPORTS & ACTIVITIES

A variety of water sports are on offer on the beach. A reef marked by buoys at the north end of the bay is suitable for snorkelling. At the beginning and end of the rainy season, Kata's surfers get on their boards. At *Phuket Surf (www.phuketsurf.com)* you can hire a board and take surfing lessons.

ENTERTAINMENT

The nightlife revolves around bars serving beer on the road from the *Kata Centre* towards Kata Noi. *Angus O'Tool's Irish Pub* in Soi Centara Karon entices with draft beers and occasional live concerts. Bob Marley would have felt at home in the atmospheric INSIDER TIP *Ska Bar* at the south end of the beach (near the Boathouse resort). The beer bars in the Bangla and Karon Plaza are mainly frequented by male travellers looking to flirt and pick up young girls telling them how handsome they are.

WHERE TO STAY

FOTO HOTEL

Modern designer hotel set back in the hillside (the property also has a free shuttle service to the beach three times a day). Spacious rooms with comfortable interior furnishings; the rooms with a sea view ("Ocean Hall") are the best option. Rooftop terrace with fantastic views, pool, WiFi at a cost. *79 rooms | 218/9 Koktanod Rd. | tel. 076 68 09 00 | www.fotohotel phuket.com | Moderate*

KATA GARDEN RESORT

Clean bungalows and rooms in a hotel with air-conditioning and minibar in a well-tended garden with pool on the hill between Kata and Karon. The walk to the beaches takes just under ten minutes. *63 rooms | 32 Karon Rd. | tel. 076 33 06 27 | www.katagardenphuket.com | Moderate–Expensive*

ORCHIDACEA RESORT

Set on a hill overlooking the sea, this tiered-terrace resort spoils its guests with affordable luxury and great views. Those who don't want to walk down to the beach can remain at the poolside. *149 rooms | 210 Khoktanod Rd. | tel. 076 28 40 83 | www.orchidacearesort.com | Moderate–Expensive*

PHUKET KATA RESORT

Tastefully decorated rooms in five standards are nestled around a large swimming pool – some with direct pool access from the veranda. 300 m/328 yds to the beach! *105 rooms | 30/9 Kata Rd. | tel. 076 33 05 81 | www.phuketkataresort.net | Moderate*

SAWASDEE VILLAGE

At the heart of this romantic, well-established resort is the pool surrounded by plants and decorative elements in traditional Thai style. With restaurant, spa and cookery courses. 40 rooms with garden view, 14 villas with direct poolside access. *38 Katekwan Rd. | tel. 076 33 09 79 | www. phuketsawasdee.com | Expensive*

LAYAN BEACH

(116 A6) (*Ø C6*) On the hills inland from this beach between Nai Thon and Bang Tao many luxury apartments and holiday homes have been built.
Phuket's ultimate exclusive resort lies on the wooded *Cape Laem Son*.

WHERE TO STAY

TRISARA ★

Luxury resort above a small nameless beach of fine-grained sand (stony at low water) with 39 villas, generously spaced across 70,000 m²/17 acres of green hilly country. Lots of wood and marble, each house has a pool and sea view. *60/1 Moo 6 | Srisoonthorn Rd. | Choeng Thale | tel. 076 31 01 00 | www.trisara.com | Expensive*

MAI KHAO BEACH

(116 A–B3) (*Ø C3*) Phuket's longest beach (10 km/6 miles) in the north was the last to be developed for tourism.
The few resorts are still spaced well apart here, and there is no danger of this beach being completely built up, as

much of the terrain is part of the Sirinat National Park. There are neither loungers nor pubs nor souvenir shops on this beach. It is perfect for those who like long, lonely walks along the sand.

SIGHTSEEING

INSIDER TIP MANGROVE JUNGLE ● ◉ (116 A1) (🗺 C1–2)

At the north end of the beach at the Sirinat National Park visitor's centre, you can take a stroll through a mangrove jungle along a wooden plank walkway and with a bit of luck you might spot a monitor lizard. The entrance to the visitor centre lies on the old road to the mainland (right), approx. 1 km/half a mile before you reach Sarasin Bridge, which is no longer open to traffic. *Daily 8.30am–4.30pm | free admission | www. dnp.go.th (for all national parks)*

FOOD & DRINK

In the little *Turtle Village* shopping centre next to the Anantara Resort you can get ice cream at *Swensens*, beer at the *Bill*

Bentley Pub, western and Thai dishes at the *Coffee Club*.

SHOPPING

You will find several high-class boutiques in *Turtle Village*, for example Jim Thompson, Esprit, Tara Leather, Triumph or J & P Gems.

WHERE TO STAY

INSIDER TIP MAI KHAO BEACH BUNGALOW

The lowest-priced resort on the whole beach by a long way. The bungalows are simply furnished but clean and have air-conditioning or a fan. The restaurant serves good Thai food, and you can have a massage beneath a canopy of palm fronds. *6 rooms | Mai Khao (near the Holiday Inn) | tel. 0818 95 12 33 | www. maikhaobeach.wordpress.com | Budget–Moderate*

MARRIOT'S MAI KHAO BEACH ◉

One of Phuket's top resorts, with superb restaurants, a gym, tennis courts, three

A sea of flowers: a fragrant bath in the spa of the Marriott's Mai Khao Beach luxury resort

pools and the island's biggest ● health and beauty spa offering numerous arrangements from a blossom bath to packages for couples. The resort makes an effort to protect the turtles that lay their eggs on Mai Khao between November and February. *265 rooms | Mai Khao | tel. 076 33 80 00 | www.marriott.com | Expensive*

INSIDER TIP RENAISSANCE PHUKET RESORT & SPA

Everything is of the finest quality in this luxury resort between the beach and an artificial lake. Pool, spa and gym, as well as yoga courses on the beach. Three restaurants, a café, a pub. In the Kids Club younger guests can run around under the supervision of trained staff or devote themselves to Playstations. *180 rooms | Mai Khao | tel. 076 36 39 99 | www.renaissancephuket. com | Expensive*

INSIDER TIP SALA PHUKET

Very trendy and characterised by simple elegance. Luxurious houses, three pools and spa. *79 rooms | Mai Khao | tel. 076 33 88 88 | www.salaphuket.com | Expensive*

NAI THON BEACH

(116 A5) *(𝄜 B–C5)* **Water buffalo still pasture behind the beach of fine-grained sand, but Nai Thon is slowly awakening from its slumber.**

A few small resorts and one large hotel have now sprung up along the beach road, and several restaurants and shops have appeared for the benefit of holidaymakers, but Nai Thon is still one of the quietest beaches on Phuket, and few day trippers come here, as it is some distance away from the main tourist centres.

FOOD & DRINK

A few beach pubs serve simple meals and drinks. For good Thai meals, head for *Tien Seng* on the beach road.

WHERE TO STAY

None of the resorts are situated directly on the beach, so wherever you are staying, you cross a quiet road to get down to the sea.

THE ANGEL OF NAITHON

A cosy complex with rustic charm. Comfortable wooden bungalows plus rooms in a building around the pool. Even if you do not stay here, it is worth looking in to see the veteran Volkswagen Beetles. The owner, Mr Miyos, collects them and is happy to stop for a chat. *10 rooms | Nai Thon Beach | tel. 08 18 30 96 28 | www.angelofnaithon. com | Moderate–Expensive*

NAITHONBURI BEACH RESORT

This three-storey building around a pool used to be the best accommodation on Nai Thon Beach. *232 rooms | Nai Thon Beach | tel. 076 31 87 00 | www.naithon buri.com | Expensive*

PULLMANN PHUKET ARCADIA

This contemporary and stylishly designed luxury resort subtly blends into the hillside and, in terms of comfort and service, leaves nothing to be desired. You have the choice between several restaurants and two pools. *277 rooms | at the northern end of the bay | tel. 076 30 32 99 | www.pullmann phuketarcadia.com | Expensive*

INSIDERTIP ▶ HIN KRUAI ●
(118 A1) (*𝑚 B6*)

The name of this little bay means "banana rock" – and so the beach has to be Banana Beach. A little paradise, not built up, with snow-white sand and a blue sea. You can get snacks and drinks in a beach bar, but it is perfectly possible, even in the high season, that only you and a few others leave footprints in the sand here. On many maps the bay is not even marked and it is easy to overlook, as you cannot see it from the road. When you drive towards Patong from Nai Thon Beach, after approx. 1 km/half a mile look out for a weathered sign (Banana Beach) by the roadside. A path leads down to the beach through dense vegetation.

NAI YANG BEACH

(116 A4) (*𝑚 C4*) **Woods of long-needled casuarinas extend between the sea and rubber plantations. In the jungle-covered hills further inland, wild boar roam through the undergrowth.**
This beach is ideal for families and nature lovers. Close to the airport, Nai Yang Beach, which is 2 km/1.25 miles long, merges with the 10 km/6-mile-long Mai Khao Beach. Accommodation directly on the beach is available only in a few resorts and in the spartan bungalows managed by the national park.
The few options for staying in Nai Yang are several minutes' walk from the beach. Offshore coral reefs forming a natural breakwater, and the shallow waters of Nai Yang Beach ensure that swimming is not dangerous even in the

Calorie bomb made of glutinous rice: a food stand on a market in Nai Yang

monsoon season, as it is on many other beaches.

SIRINAT NATIONAL PARK ⊘
The whole of Nai Yang Beach is officially part of Sirinat National Park, marked as Nai Yang National Park on many maps. The northern part of the beach has not been built up. The small museum run by the national park authority informs visitors about the fauna of the area, with exhibitions of shells, corals and insects. *Daily 8.30am–noon and 1pm–4.30pm | the museum is free, but foreigners have to pay 200 baht admission to enter the*

park. It costs 30 baht extra to drive through in your car | www.dnp.go.th

FOOD & DRINK

Many food stalls and open-air restaurants. The shady trees make Nai Yang a popular picnic spot for the Thais.

INSIDER TIP ▶ RIVET GRILL

Those in the know make the journey from the south of the island up here to the north for Sunday brunch in this restaurant, which belongs to *The Slate*. Sushi, steaks, pasta, oysters, bread, cheese and cake, cost from 2,050 baht, with soft drinks or 2,550 baht with wine or, for more extravagance, 4,050 baht with champagne. Under 7s go free while 7–14 year olds pay the half. *Daily dinner, brunch Sun noon–3.30pm (booking recommended) | tel. 076 32 70 06 | Moderate–Expensive*

SPORTS & ACTIVITIES

PHUKET KITE SCHOOL

From May until late October you can learn how to zoom across the waves, pulled by a steerable kite. A three-hour beginner's course costs 3,500 baht. *Beach Rd. | tel. 08 00 77 75 94 | www.kiteschoolphuket.com.* For the rest of the year, the school moves across to the bay of Chalong *(Wiset Rd.)*, because the wind is better there in this period.

WHERE TO STAY

DANG SEA BEACH BUNGALOW

These bungalows are located beneath casuarina trees in the middle of the beach. Basic but well-kept, with air-conditioning, TV, refrigerator. Plenty of little beach cafés nearby. *10 rooms | Nai Yang Beach | tel. 076 32 83 62 | Moderate*

SEAPINES VILLA LIBERG

This cosy resort is located between the beach and village and is surrounded by a large wall – creating a world on its own. The individualised rooms are all designed in Thai style. There are also three small villas for families. *16 rooms | 11 Moo 5, behind The Slate | tel. 08 18 14 48 83 | Budget*

THE SLATE

This top-quality resort boasts a postmodern architecture serving as a reminder of the tin mining times. Spa, three pools, two tennis courts, four restaurants. Those who like it romantic can dine right on the beach in the evenings. Courses in yoga, Pilates and Thai kick-boxing. *290 rooms | Nai Yang Beach | tel. 076 32 70 06 | www.theslatephuket.com | Expensive*

PANSEA BEACH

(118 A3) *(🔗 B7–8)* **This small bay is separated from Bang Tao by a wooded rocky headland and sheltered by the slopes of a hill right behind the beach.** Pansea Beach is a world of its own. Which is appreciated by guests at two luxury resorts, *Amanpuri* and *The Surin*, situated high above the sea.

FOOD & DRINK

The restaurants of the high-class resorts on Pansea Beach are excellent – but unfortunately fairly expensive. The beach bars and eateries in the hinterland of *Surin Beach* are cheaper, and it takes only ten minutes to walk there.

World-class: international stars take holidays at the Amanpuri Beach resort

WHERE TO STAY

AMANPURI

Beautiful bungalows in classic Thai style. Even though it is no longer brand new, Amanpuri is still right up there in the world league of top resorts, as the presence of celebrities such as Robert de Niro confirms. You will not be disappointed, providing you are able to pay 800 euros per night for the pleasure. *40 rooms | 118 Srisoonthorn Rd. | tel. 076 32 43 33 | www. aman.com/resorts/amanpuri | Expensive*

THE SURIN

Popular top-class hotel with excellent service. Nice spot on a wooded slope, but with some stairs to negotiate. Shingle-roofed luxury bungalows in grey-and-white retro design. Not quite so elite as in the Amanpuri next door, but then The Surin is significantly cheaper (from approx. 300 euros). The black-tiled octagonal pool is a real eye-catcher. *103 rooms | 118 Srisoonthorn Rd. | tel. 076 62 15 80 | www.thesurinphuket.com | Expensive*

PATONG BEACH

MAP ON PAGE 51

(120 A–B2) *(ᗰ C10)* **In the 1970s globetrotters stayed here in bamboo huts. Now hotels occupy the site, and a town is spreading where boys herded water buffalo as late as the 1980s.** Patong has turned into what many tourists want to see: a great big noisy place of entertainment. Whether you are looking for a bar, a boutique or your favourite meals from back home

– here you will find all of these things. The 3 km/2-mile-long beach is crowded.

In the centre of this tourist town, masses of visitors throng the stores, tailors' shops, street stalls and restaurants. Loud music emanates from hundreds of bars, and an army of girls, boys and *ladyboys* (transvestites and transsexuals) lie in wait for men to spend the night with – or the rest of their life. Patong Beach is no finishing school for posh girls, but a place where sailors come looking for some fun. Indeed, ships of the US Navy sometimes anchor in the bay. You will not find any of Phuket's top-class resort hotels here, but slowly things are changing. The first carefully designed clubs are adding a bit of quality to the nightlife, and some chic restaurants and a few stylish boutique resorts have opened here.

FOOD & DRINK

There is an enormous choice here. International or Thai food, low-cost or exclusive – Patong Beach has something for every taste and budget. The food prepared on street stalls is the best value for money, and often the tastiest you will get. Many INSIDER TIP mobile cooks can be found from late afternoon along the wall of the Muslim cemetery in the middle of the beach.

BAAN RIM PA

The veteran of Patong's top restaurants, at the north end of town, is still excellent. Piano music forms the accompaniment to royal Thai cuisine, which means that the ingredients are as fresh as can be and that the dishes are presented with artistic flair – a treat for the eyes and the palate. *Daily lunch/dinner | 223*

Hot pot: The chef grabs a handful of seafood to throw into the wok at Patong Beach

Laem Daeng

Kalim Beach

Nerntong Resort

The Orchid Gh.
Ban Kalim

Blue Marine   Patong Lodge

Diamond Cliff

Da Maurizio

Novotel

Baan Rim Pa

Ao

Phra

Wong Road

A. A. Villa   Barami
Sunset Mansion   P. S. II
Penthouse   Bungalow   Road
Eden   Nordic

Patong Beach

Muslim Cemetery

Swiss Palm
Beach
Andaman
Beach
Suites

New Tum
Bungalows

Patong

Boomerang Inn

Patong Beach
Road   Patong Bayshore

Impiana Resort

Playhouse   Patong City

Thara

Patong
Boxing Stadium

Sai Nam
Yen
Road

La Flora
Bay Garden Resort

Bay Inn   Neptuna

Wong Road

Safari   Patong
Villa

Royal Paradise

Tropica   Bangla Road

Patong Inn

Baan Sand
Sukothai Inn   P. S. I.
Aloha Villa   Expat Hotel
Soi Saen
Sabai

Rachauthit Road

PATONG

Ban Thai
Cosmos Inn   Patong
Resort

Sea Sun
Sand
Holiday

Baipho

Montana Grand

Thawi Soi Aloha

Absolut
Seagull Cottage   Merlin
Villa del Mar   Holiday
Quality Inn   Resort
Baan Bou   Swiss
Seaview   Duangjit   Thamdee Inn
Lydia's   Resort

The Golden Land Plaza

Baumanburi

Thaweewong Road   Soi Song

Coconut
Cottage

Coconut
Village

Na   Nai   Road

Phuket Palace

Club Bamboo

Trai Trang

500 m
547 yd

© Bernation Productions GmbH

Kalim Beach Rd. | tel. 076 34 07 89 | www.baanrimpa.com | *Moderate–Expensive*

JOE'S DOWNSTAIRS ●

As the name says, you go down steps from the street, and enter a joint just above the water where everything is white. This is a lovely place to sip a sundowner. The food is New World cuisine, ranging from a Portobello burger to rock lobster with mango. *Daily lunch/dinner | 223/3 Kalim Beach Rd. | next to Baan Rim Pa | tel. 076 34 42 54 | www.joes phuket.com | Expensive*

THE 9TH FLOOR

Swiss sausage salad and steaks, Thai prawn soup and risotto. Normally this kind of crazy mixture sets off the alarm bells, but here the quality is truly good, and the view from the ❄ open-air restaurant on the ninth floor is a winner. *Daily 6pm–midnight | 47 Rat Uthit Rd. | in the Sky Inn Condotel | tel. 076 34 43 11 | www.the9thfloor.com | Moderate–Expensive*

INSIDER TIP PUM RESTAURANT

Classic, down-to-earth Thai cooking such as fried noodles and curry is on the menu here. You can watch the cooks at work in this open restaurant. And in ● *Pum's Cooking School* you can put on the chef's apron yourself. *Daily 11am–9pm | 204/32 Rat Uthit Rd. | next to Christine Massage |* tel. 076 34 62 69 | www.pumthaifoodchain.com | *Budget*

SALA BUA

Out-of-the-ordinary creations such as duck ravioli as well as classic Thai dishes such as green curry with chicken are served in this eatery. Diners enjoy this delicious food right on the beach in the *Impiana* resort. *Daily from noon | 41 Taweewong Rd. | tel. 076 34 01 38 | Expensive*

SHOPPING

Shops, stalls, countless street traders – and in spite of all of this, it is difficult to find anything original, as the offerings consist of souvenir tat and copied products. The biggest shopping centre with more than 300 shops and restaurants, is ● *Jungceylon (www.jungceylon.com)* on *Ra Uthit Rd.* Alongside bars and food stalls, the INSIDER TIP *OTOP Shopping Paradise (same road, opposite Hard Rock Café)* also sells beautiful handicraft products made all over Thailand.

SPORTS & ACTIVITIES

You can try your hand at a wide range of sports and activities at Patong Beach and more inland.

INSIDER TIP FLYING HANUMAN

If sliding through the jungle at a hair-raising speed and height attached to a wire rope sounds like fun to you, then you've come to the right address. It also appeals to children in search of adventure. And don't worry; the guides in the park are extremely vigilant when it comes to safety. Although the zipline is situated deep in the jungle far away from the beaten track on the way to the Kathu Waterfall, there is a shuttle service avail-

LOW BUDGET

There is an endless number of small hotels which offer rooms from 600 baht perfect for those travelling on a shoestring; for example the *Seabreeze Inn* in Karon. *13 rooms | 526/23-24 Patak Rd. | tel. 076 39 69 31*

In the centre of Kata in a quiet location just ten minutes from the beach is the *Fantasy Hill Bungalow*. Rooms with air-conditioning and TV cost 1200 baht with rooms with ventilator only for 650 baht. *34 rooms | Kata Beach | 8/1 Karon Rd. | tel. 076 33 01 06 | www.sites.google.com/site/fantasyhillbungalow*

At Patong Beach, good traditional food is sold for just a few baht at the food stalls lining the narrow street off from Bangla Road near the *Heroes Bar*.

able to visitors. *Daily 8am–5pm | 89/16 Moo 6 | Soi Namtok Kathu | tel. 076 32 32 64 | flyinghanuman.com*

PATONG GO-KART SPEEDWAY

Do you have petrol running through your veins and the smell of burnt rubber gets your adrenalin racing? Then drive a few rounds of the track in the go-karts which are parked along the road to Phuket Town. *Daily 10am–10pm | tel. 076 32 19 49 | gokartthailand.com*

SF STRIKE BOWL

This is not the place if you're looking for a quiet afternoon pastime – bowling is loud and raucous fun for the whole family and the perfect action for a rainy day. *Daily 10am–10pm | at the Jungceylon Center, 3rd floor | Tel. 076 60 03 34*

WATER SPORTS & DIVING

Splashing around in the water can be fun in itself but if you're looking for a bit more action then head to the beach with its wide range of activities from paragliding, jet-skiing, banana boating or diving. There are several diving centres which offer courses and longer diving excursions. More information is available at *Santana Diving Shop (daily 10am–noon and 4–10pm | 74/26 Soi Banzaan | tel. 076 60 88 44 | www.santanaphuket. com).*

ENTERTAINMENT

The epicentre of nightlife is around ● *Bangla Road* and its side streets. Soi Seadragon, Soi Tiger and Soi Freedom are all lined with one beer bar after the next and endless go-go bars wait expectantly for customers. On or close to these amusement miles are some of the island's biggest clubs, some of which are exclusive establishments where international DJs perform.

Feel the wind in your hair: paragliding along the sea at Patong Beach

ILLUZION CLUB & DISCO
This venue has tapped into the trend of organising DJ gigs as well as Las Vegas-style shows often performing to a sold-out crowd. Take a look at the party photos on its Facebook page: as you'll see, the club attracts a young and sexy audience. *Daily 10pm–4am | admission varies depending on events and day of the week | 31 Bangla Rd. | tel. 076 68 30 30 | www.illuzionphuket.com*

INSIDER TIP ▶ MOLLY MALONE'S
Are you a man? And are you looking for a place for a quiet pint without being hit on by women telling you how handsome you are? Then this Irish Pub is the right address, serving decent food and with its own rock band. *Daily 10am–2am | 94/1 Thawiwong Rd. | tel. 07 62 92 77 12*

SEDUCTION NIGHTCLUB
The largest disco at Patong Beach is located on the 2nd floor of the five-storey nightlife complex. The venue accommodates up to 3000 people who come to hear the latest sounds from the coolest DJs around. *Daily 10pm–4am | admission varies depending on events and day of the week | eastern end of Bangla Rd. | tel. 076 34 31 73 | www.seductiondisco.com*

SIMON CABARET ★
This transvestite show has been going strong since 1991 but don't worry; new performers appear every year who come to showcase their tailor-made costumes (and bodies). There are three shows every evening.Daily *6pm, 7.30 and 9 pm | admission 800–1000 baht | 8 Sirirat Rd. | tel. 076 34 20 14 | phuket-simoncabaret.com*

PATONG BOXING STADIUM
Fists are flying here in the *Sainamyen* stadium where you can join the audience to watch real Thai boxing fights. Professional Thai boxers meet head to head who can really pack a punch. Nothing for the faint hearted! *Mon, Thu and Sun from 9pm | admission 1300–1800 baht | Sainamyen Rd. | boxingstadiumpatong.com*

WHERE TO STAY

Not many hotels are situated right on the beach. Please bear in mind that it is not acceptable in Thailand to walk to the beach through the streets wearing swimming shorts or a bikini.

INSIDER TIP ▶ BAIPHO
This little gem of a boutique hotel lies hidden in a side street leading to the *Montana Grand* hotel. Swiss fashion photographer Rudi Horber has styled it from top to bottom, from the indirect lighting to the works of art on the walls. Air-conditioning, minibar, DVD players, and use of the *Montana Grand's* pool. Ten minutes to the beach. *19 rooms | 205/12–13 Rat Uthit Rd. | tel. 076 29 20 74 | www.baipho.com | Moderate*

BOOMERANG INN
Plain, clean rooms in this three-storey guesthouse with a small pool are equipped with TV, minibar and air-conditioning. Central location, five minutes from the beach. *61 rooms | 5/1–8 Hat Patong Rd. (Patong Beach Rd.) | tel. 076 34 21 82 | www.boomeranginn.com | Budget–Moderate*

DUANGJITT RESORT
Hotel and bungalow complex scattered in a large park. Three pools, spa. At the quieter south end of Patong Beach. Three minutes to the beach. *508 rooms | 18 Phachanukhork Rd. | tel. 076 34 07 78 | www.duangjittresort-spa.com | Expensive*

A blaze of colour: the transvestite show at Simon Cabaret

ORCHID RESIDENCE

Cosy guesthouse with air-conditioning, TV, DVD players, refrigerators in the rooms. Seven minutes from the beach. *16 rooms | 171 Soi Sansabai | tel. 076 34 51 76 | www.orchid-residence.com | Budget-Moderate*

ROYAL PHAWADEE VILLAGE

A tropical garden with trees surrounds this charming resort. Wooden houses in the style of north Thailand with balcony, air-conditioning, TV. Pool beneath palms, five minutes to the beach. *36 rooms | 3 Sawatdirak Rd. | tel. 076 34 46 22 | www.royal-phawadee-village. com | Expensive*

TROPICA

You only have to cross the road to get to the beach, and the bar district is round the corner – this resort has a very central location, but with its lushly planted garden nevertheless forms a green oasis in the middle of all the action. Rooms in a two-storey building or bungalows clustering around a pool. All rooms with air-conditioning, refrigerator and TV. *86 rooms | 132 Thaweewong Rd. at the corner of Soi Bangla | tel. 076 34 02 04 | www.tropica-bungalow.com | Expensive*

WHERE TO GO

FREEDOM BEACH (120 A3) (*ⓜ B11*)

At the south end of Patong Beach long-tails set off from a floating pier to take day trippers an a 30-minute voyage around a headland to picturesque Free-dom Beach *(return journey approx. 1200 baht incl. waiting time | admission 100 baht)*. There are no hotels there, only a basic restaurant. Compared to Patong, Freedom Beach is quiet and relaxing. The water is clear enough for

Freedom Beach: a sandy beach and a nice view, not just for snorkellers

snorkelling, the sand is fine-grained. On the way there you pass *Paradise Beach*, also known as *Diamond Beach*, which is quieter but equally beautiful.

SURIN BEACH

(118 A3) (*ⵑ C8*) **Surin Beach, about 500 m/547 yd long, has been transformed from a place for water buffalo into a luxury beach.**

The hills behind Surin Beach are gradually being built up with fine homes. On the main road classy boutiques in *Plaza* cater for wealthy customers. But low-cost accommodation can still be found, as well as peace and quiet.

FOOD & DRINK

Although there are no more bars directly on the beach, simply head a few 100 metres inland for a wide choice of sophisticated or basic food and snacks.

BLUE LAGOON
Basic, family-run restaurant serving authentic Thai food especially seafood. Sit at one of the tables overlooking the busy main road to occupy you while you wait for your food (which can take a while). *Daily 8am–11pm | 4025 Choeng Thalay | tel. 08 79 23 82 35 | Budget*

THE 9TH GLASS WINE BAR & BISTRO
A fine-dining establishment with over 160 excellent wines from around the world to choose from as well as delicious tapas style snacks conjured up by star chef Anthony. Popular main meals include the sirloin steak or extremely tender salmon. Advisable to book in advance. *Mon–Sat 4pm–midnight | 106/16 Moo 3 | Surin Beach Rd. | tel. 06 20 68 00 68 | the9thglass.com | Moderate–Expensive*

SURIN CHILL HOUSE
Tiny restaurant with authentic Thai cuisine and the 'usual suspects' on a sepa-

rate menu with international dishes. An affordable and good place to eat. *Daily 8.30am–11pm | 107/3 Moo 3 | Surin Beach Rd. | tel. 076 63 62 54 | www. tastesurinbeach.com | Budget–Moderate*

SHOPPING

The Plaza Surin on the main road is an upmarket shopping centre where the owners of villas in this area come to look for furniture, art and antiques. *Soul of Asia*, one of the island's best antique shops, is based here. Clothes and a better quality of souvenirs are also sold here. A short distance away you can buy European wines from the *Central Wine Cellar*. Next door at *C Bakery* you can find bread, croissants and other baked goods.

SPORTS & ACTIVITIES

INSIDERTIP DE SURIN HEALTH SPA
Have you ever had a hollow bamboo cane massage before? Located on the 2nd floor of The *Plaza Surin* shopping centre, this tiny, exclusive spa promises a deeper and firmer massage experience which is the ultimate in relaxation. *Daily 10am–10pm | 5/50 2nd Floor Room #M1, Moo 3 | tel. 09 50 93 22 88 | www.desurin. com*

WHERE TO STAY

BENYADA LODGE
Elegant boutique hotel with simple design. Rooms have air-conditioning, TV and minibar. Roof terrace with bar and loungers for sunbathing. Only two minutes to the beach. *29 rooms | Surin Beach | tel. 076 27 12 61 | www.benyada lodge-phuket.com | Moderate*

SURIN BAY INN
A friendly place, only three minutes' walk from the beach. When you stand on the ☼ balcony of your room, the view extends to the whole bay. Well-kept rooms with air-conditioning, TV, refrigerator, and excellent value for money by the standards of expensive Surin Beach. *12 rooms | Surin Beach | tel. 076 27 16 01 | Moderate*

SURIN SWEET HOTEL
Large, clean rooms with air-conditioning, balcony, refrigerator, TV. Pool. Alongside Thai dishes, the restaurant also serves Italian food. The manager Marco comes from Italy which you'll notice when you try his pizzas. *30 rooms | Surin Beach | tel. 076 27 08 63 | surinsweetho tel.com | Moderate*

TWIN PALMS
Top resort, to design from top to bottom. Luxurious rooms, some with their own pool. Day trips to Phang Nga Bay on the resort's own chic yacht. *76 rooms | Surin Beach | tel. 076 31 65 00 | www.twin palms-phuket.com | Expensive*

WHERE TO GO

LAEM SINGH ☼
(118 A3) (*C8*)
At the Lion Cape, 1.5 km/1 mile south of Surin on the road towards Patong Beach, what may be the most scenically beautiful bay on Phuket is situated below the road: rocks as on the Seychelles, and a little stream that flows from the foot of the green hills across the fine sand of the beach into the sea. As it is near to Patong Beach, a lot of motorboats come here, and the beach is always busy. There are no hotels, but several beach restaurants. Parking spaces are available up on the road.

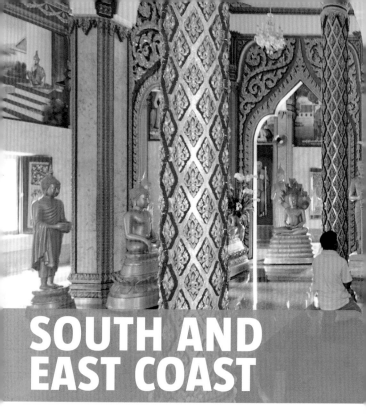

SOUTH AND EAST COAST

Although the capital of Phuket lies on the east coast, outside the town little has been changed by tourism. Which is why the east coast is a popular residential area for expatriates who live on Phuket.

Most of the beaches are muddy and stony. Mangrove swamps and farms for prawns and crabs line the coast. To the south of the harbour of Phuket however, beyond Cape Phan Wa, and in the bay of Chalong, adventurous holidaymakers will find acceptable beaches. Above all, the area inland from here remains largely authentic. And in the far south there are even two picturesque bays and a fantastic beach.

AO CHALONG

(120–121 C–D 4–5) (*M E–F12*) **The bay of Chalong is a popular point of anchorage for sailing yachts from all over the world, which find shelter from the monsoon storms here.**

Fisherman land their catch, and in the backcountry goats graze in plantations of coconut palms. Only a few miles south of the pier, *Mittrapab (Friendship) Beach* and *Laem Ka Beach* are clean, but swimming is only possible at high tide. Roads lead down to the water and to the few places to stay. It is also possible to take a boat out to the offshore islands. If you are looking for peace and quiet and have a car or moped, you will be content here.

Few tourists – but more authentic, with a lot of nature, everyday village life and stunning sunsets

BIG BUDDHA ★ ☼

While the whole site has not yet been completed – it is financed entirely by donations –, with a height of 45 m/150 ft, the enormous Buddha at an altitude of 400 m/1300 ft on Nagakerd Mountain is already an overwhelming sight. The views are fantastic in all directions. *Daily 6am–7pm | admission free | shortly after Chalong on the main road towards the airport;* *turn-off signposted | www.phuket-big-buddha.com*

WAT CHALONG ★ ●

3 km/2 miles north of the roundabout in the village of Chalong, on the by-pass road to the airport, the red roofs of the largest Buddhist monastery on Phuket shine in the sun. A big fair is held here every year at Chinese New Year. Visitors set off fireworks all year to give thanks for wishes which have come true over the year. *Admission free*

FOOD & DRINK

DICKIES LIGHTHOUSE RESTAURANT AND BAR

Their burgers are popular with hungry sailors. *Daily from 10am | left of Chalong pier | tel. 076 38 30 45 | www.dickieslight house.com | Moderate*

Staying on Ao Sane Beach – as romantic as it gets and very rustic

KANG EANG

A beautiful sight in the evenings when the lights reflect in the water. *Daily from 11 am | directly on the pier | tel. 076 38 12 12 | www.kaneang-pier.com | Moderate–Expensive*

INSIDER TIP PALAI SEAFOOD

Located directly at the beach, 1km/half a mile after Phuket Zoo. This almost tourist-free restaurant serves extremely tasty food. *Daily from 10am | tel. 076 28 21 74 | Moderate–Expensive*

SPORTS & ACTIVITIES

On the edge of Chalong, a whole row of leisure facilities have opened on the road towards Kata Beach *(all daily 9am–6pm)*. At *Phuket Shooting Range* you can take aim at targets or clay pigeons. At *Paintball,* visitors shoot at each other with (harmless) paint bullets.

WHERE TO STAY

FRIENDSHIP BEACH RESORT

This veteran among resorts on Phuket, halfway between Chalong and Rawai, is popular with long-term guests. Rooms, apartments, bungalows with every amenity. Pool by the sea. Good yoga courses. *40 rooms | Soi Mittrapab | tel. 076 28 89 96 | www.friendshipbeach. com | Expensive*

SHANTI LODGE

Small, well-run establishment in a quiet side street. With a seawater pool and restaurant; choose between air-conditioning or fan. *14 rooms | 1/2 Soi Bangrae | Choafa Nok Rd. | about 1 km/0.6 mile north of the Chalong roundabout on Bypass Rd. | tel. 076 28 02 33 | www. shantilodge.com | Budget*

AO SANE BEACH

(120 A–B6) *(∅ C14)* **This** INSIDER TIP **romantic rocky cove lies at the end of the road that leads from Nai Harn Beach and passes beneath the yacht club, first up and then down a hill.**

This is a little world of its own along two tiny beaches, where corals emerge from the water at low tide. For children these beaches are not suitable, as there is a risk of injury. Everything has remained in a fairly natural condition, and two resorts share this little paradise. A lot of day trippers come here, however, when they find other beaches too crowded for their taste.

SPORTS & ACTIVITIES

The only diving base on Phuket that is right by the beach is run by multilingual Armin and his team at *Ao Sane Bungalows*. You can walk to your diving baptism on the local reef. *www.armins-diveteam.com*

WHERE TO STAY

BAAN KRATING PHUKET RESORT
Spacious wooden and concrete bungalows with air-conditioning, TV and minibar beneath leafy trees. Small pool. The food is better and cheaper in the restaurant of the neighbouring *Ao Sane Bungalows*. *65 rooms | Ao Sane | tel. 076 28 82 64 | www.baankrating.com | Expensive*

LAEM PHAN WA

(121 E4) (*ΩΩ F12*) **Laem means cape, and the most beautiful beach on the east coast lies on this cape at the foot of green hills, fringed by palms.**
Guests at the resorts have this bay all to themselves. Thanks to a sheltered location, even in the monsoon season there are seldom big waves here. It is a good option for visitors who want a quiet life in comfort and close to town.

SIGHTSEEING

PHUKET AQUARIUM ★ ●
There is a lot to discover under water by snorkelling at Phuket's beaches – but to see the big catches up close, such as a shark and a manta ray, you'll have to visit the *Phuket Aquarium.* The plethora of Phuket's sea life can be seen here from tiny, neon-coloured coral fish to poisonous lion fish. *Daily 8.30am–4pm | admission 100 baht | Sakdidet Rd. | www.phuketaquarium.org*

FOOD & DRINK

PANWA HOUSE
This enchanting white house looks like the residence of a tin magnate. Thai food is served right on the beach. *Tue–Sun dinner | in the Cape Panwa Hotel | tel. 076 39 11 23 | Moderate–Expensive*

★ **Big Buddha**
Thailand's tallest Buddha on the summit of a hill → p. 59

★ **Wat Chalong**
Phuket's biggest Buddhist temple hosts a fair for Chinese New Year → p. 59

★ **Phuket Aquarium**
Eyeball to eyeball with sharks and coral-reef fish → p. 61

★ **Nai Harn Beach**
A wonderful tropical bay → p. 62

★ **Laem Promthep**
Viewpoint for sunsets → p. 63

MARCO POLO HIGHLIGHTS

WHERE TO STAY

CAPE PANWA HOTEL
Luxurious rooms in the hotel building and six bungalows on the hillside. Pool, tennis courts and even a short cable lift from the hotel down to the beach. *246 rooms | Sakdidet Rd. | Cape Panwa | tel. 076 39 11 23 | www.capepanwa.com | Expensive*

NAI HARN BEACH

(120 B6) *(ᗰ C14)* ⭐ **Blue sea, a large sandy beach framed by green hill slopes, and a lagoon behind it – no wonder hippies and backpackers were particularly attached to Nai Harn Beach when tourism started up on Phuket.**

The hippies and their huts on stilts have now disappeared, but Nai Harn has not become busy and noisy. Here you will find only two resorts, as well as a few souvenir shops and open-air pubs. Most visitors are day trippers who find the beaches by their own hotels too crowded. In the high season a lot of sailing yachts anchor here.

FOOD & DRINK

Top-quality food is served in two first-class restaurants in the *The Nai Harn (both open daily for dinner | tel. 076 38 02 00 | Expensive*). Several basic open-air restaurants do business on the approach to the beach and behind the coastal promenade. For delicious cakes and good coffee, try INSIDER TIP *A Spoonful of Sugar (Tue–Sun 8am–7pm | Budget)*, a charming café with retro design on Saiyuan Rd., opposite the *Herbal Sauna.* Approx. 300 m/300 yd before you reach it, on the same side of the road, the *German Bakery (daily 7.30am–5.30pm | Budget)* sells freshly baked bread and hearty sausages. EA great place (not only) for health junkies is the nearby INSIDER TIP *Phuket Vegan (31/48 Moo 1 | tel. 08 48 37 44 29 | Moderate)*, where Mr. Chai conjures up his magical creations.

AN ALL-PURPOSE TREE

For tourists it symbolises the tropics and the desire to be in a far-away place. But for the Thais, the coconut palm is the ultimate tree. Not only for its large fruit with delicious milk that is as clear as water. The coconut palm is a source of much more. The dried flesh, copra, is made into oil and used for cooking and making soap. The hard inner part of the shell can be used to collect the latex sap from rubber trees, for example. When dry, the outer part of the shell is fuel for cooking. The straight trunk of palm trees can be sawn into boards. The palm fronds can be woven to make a roof covering that stands up to the heaviest monsoon rain, at least for a few years. And the best characteristic of this all-purpose tree is that it is not demanding, and grows as well on wet pastures as on a hot sandy beach.

Laem Promthep: this rocky cape is a popular vantage point for spectacular sunsets

SPORTS & ACTIVITIES

With a INSIDER TIP length of 2 km/1.25 miles, the promenade around the lake behind the beach is the most pleasant jogging circuit on Phuket. Don't be too surprised when passing cars and mopeds sound their horns at the point where the road branches off to Cape Promthep. This is a sign of respect for the Chinese shrine here. If you open the gate, you can enter the small building and light one of the joss sticks placed there free of charge.

WHERE TO STAY

ALL SEASONS

This resort is not right on the beach, but you only have to walk a few paces across the road. Comfortable rooms, two pools, sauna. *154 rooms | Nai Harn Beach | tel. 076 28 93 27 | www.allseasons-naiharn-phuket.com | Expensive*

THE NAI HARN ☆

The former *Royal Phuket Yacht Club* was the first 5-star hotel on the island. Each room has its own veranda with fantastic views over the bay. Although the pool is on the small side, the beach is just a stone's throw away. Non-hotel guests are also invited to enjoy a drink in the ● ☆ *Reflections Bar* and the views of the bay. Two sunset drinks are available for the price of one during happy hour between 5.30pm–6.30pm. *130 rooms | 23/3 Moo 1 | Vises Rd. | tel. 076 38 02 00 | www.thenaiharn.com | Expensive*

WHERE TO GO

LAEM PROMTHEP ★ ☆
(120 B6) (*Ⓜ C14*)

On this rocky cape, the southernmost tip of the island, whole busloads of tourists come to see the fantastic sunsets (access from Rawai and Nai Harn). From the cape *(laem)* you get a great view of the sea, the bay of Nai Harn and the island of Man. In the `INSIDER TIP` garden of the 🍴 *Promthep Cape Restaurant (tel. 076 28 86 56 | Budget)* the *Phuket Paradise Cocktail* comes recommended. The food is okay but nothing special. Be sure to book a table with sea view! There are also stalls selling cooked meals and drinks at the cape. In honour of the king, a ● lighthouse *(daily 10am–6pm/ admission free)* was built. In the air-conditioned interior you can view marine charts, as well as models of

RAWAI BEACH

(120 B–C6) (🗺 D14) Rawai Beach has never been a tourist haunt. It is simply too muddy, because the sea withdraws a long way at low tide. At least the sea cucumbers like the water here.

Still, the beach used to be popular with long-term holidaymakers, as well as among the Thais themselves. In the village of Rawai time seemed to stand still,

Fish straight from the sea is sold at the fish market on Rawai Beach

ships and sextants. It's also well worth making the trip to the `INSIDER TIP` viewing point of the 🍴 *Promthep Alternative Energy Station* on the road from Nai Harn to the cape (take the turning by the wind generator). Great views of the azure sea, tiny Ya Nui Beach and Ko Man island.

and it was possible to eat well and cheaply at the food stalls beneath the casuarina trees on the long beach – until progress arrived. A promenade (where almost nobody walks) was built and the food stalls were forced to move to the other end of the beach, where there is no shade, to the *Pakbang Food Center.* A four-lane road was constructed through the village, robbing it of almost all its character. ● On the beach, longtails are waiting to take you to the islands off the coast.

Even in the main season, the number of day trippers is not large.

FOOD & DRINK

BAAN HAD RAWAI

At the south end of Rawai Beach, Thai dishes and seafood are served in the open air. Many Thais come here to eat – which is always a good sign! *Daily | tel. 076 38 38 38 | Budget–Moderate*

FLINTS ONE BAKERY

The rolls, bread and cakes from this bakery taste delicious. It also serves sandwiches with sausage and cheese, as well as good coffee. *Daily | beach road at the junction with the Phuket Town road | tel. 076 28 92 10 | Budget*

ENTERTAINMENT

The bars *Nikita* and *Freedom* are a favoured gathering point for the small numbers of tourists and the *falang* (expats) who live here permanently.

WHERE TO STAY

THAI PALACE RESORT

The rooms and bungalows of this small, attractive resort are centred round two pools. The garden is full of flowers and plants and there are several good restaurants in the area. *58 rooms | 52/8 Moo 6 | Viset Rd. | tel. 076 28 80 42 | www.thaipalacephuket.com | Moderate*

YA NUI BEACH

(120 B6) (*∅ C14*) **A picturesque little beach in a valley halfway between Nai Harn and Promthep.**

WHERE TO STAY

INSIDER TIP **NAIYA BEACH BUNGALOWS**

Plain but attractive stilt bungalows with fans, five minutes up the hill beneath trees in well-kept grounds. All with veranda, spacious and clean. The restaurant serves breakfast and snacks. *20 rooms | open Nov–April | 99 Soi Ya Nui | Viset Rd. | tel. 076 28 88 17 | www.naiya beachbungalow.com | Budget*

LOW BUDGET

The *Ao Sane Bungalows* in the bay of Ao Sane with their bamboo huts on stilts are a reminder of the hippie era (300 baht with shower). Even the bungalows with fans all cost less than 1000 baht. Many regular guests, dive centre, excellent food. *23 rooms | Ao Sane | tel. 076 28 83 06*

Breakfast for 30 baht: *Kanom Chin*, rice noodles with curry sauce, with raw and pickled vegetables are served in a nameless eatery (*Fri–Wed 7am–11am*). When you come up from Nai Harn, turn left into Sai Yuan Rd. you'll find it on the right after approx. 150 m/165 yds (opposite Didi's Hair Salon). But don't expect anyone to speak English here!

On The Rock: 17 rooms with fan or air-conditioning for 800 to 1200 baht. Behind *The Nai Harn* resort. Two minutes' walk to Nai Harn Beach. *Tel. 08 69 52 08 19.*

PHUKET TOWN

 MAP INSIDE BACK COVER
(121 D–E 2–3) (*E–F 10–11*)

While Phuket Town is the capital of the island province, it is far from being a provincial town.

Whereas in other districts the old wooden houses gave way to concrete blocks long ago, in *Old Phuket Town*, the centre of Phuket Town, many buildings in the so-called Sino-Portuguese style have remained. Showing the signs of time and the tropical climate, they contribute to the charm of this bustling town of 70,000 inhabitants.

Of course the modern construction boom and tourism have made their mark, and visitors who leave the beach for a few hours in the daytime to come to town often fail to notice that the old Phuket is still alive, only one street away from the faceless new buildings and souvenir shops. However, if you take a little time and look in the nooks and crannies, you will discover many details that add up to a likeable overall picture.

SIGHTSEEING

JUI TUI TEMPLE ★ ●
(U A3–4) (*a3–4*)

This Chinese Taoist temple at the corner of Ranong Rd. and Soi Phu Thon is dedicated to the vegetarian god Kiu Wong In and is the site of many ceremonies during the *Vegetarian Festival*. The roofs of next door's *Kwan Im Teng* (sometimes called *Put Jaw*), also a Taoist temple, are adorned with rampant dragons. It is

Old townhouses in the Sino-Portuguese style, lots of restaurants, folklore and a host of little shops – Phuket Town has plenty of variety

dedicated to the goddess of mercy, and dates back 200 years, which makes it Phuket's oldest Chinese temple. *Free admission*

OLD PHUKET TOWN ★ ●
(U B3) *(Ш b3)*

No other city in Thailand possesses so much old architecture with colonial charm as Phuket Town. Chinese immigrants from neighbouring Malaysia brought the Sino-Portuguese style with them. North of the roundabout near to

WHERE TO START?
Roundabout **(U B3–4)**
(Ш b3–4): Bangkok Rd., Ranong Rd., Yaowaraj Rd. and Rasada Rd. meet at the central roundabout. The public buses and pickups from the beaches arrive here. Go left to the market, head north and you'll soon find yourself in the middle of the old quarter. Going right will take you to the shopping district.

Historic photos in the Thaihua Museum: Chinese migrants shaped the city's past and present

the central market, the old quarter is full of shop buildings with stucco decorations. The ground floors are for business, and whole families live above. In *Thalang Road* in particular you are strolling through the architectural history of the town. Fine examples of sensitive restoration of the old building fabric can be seen in the side street *Soi Rommani*. The imposing townhouses of the old tin magnates are to be found along *Krabi Road*, for example. The outstanding example here is *Phra Pitak Chinpracha Mansion*, which is over 100 years old. Following an elaborate restoration, it now houses the restaurant *Blue Elephant* (see p. 69).

RANG HILL ★ ☀ (U A1–2) (*⽥ a1–2*)
The Thai name for the hill that overlooks Phuket Town on its northwestern side is *Khao Rang* (access via *Kho Simbi Rd.* or *Soi Wachira*). Its height may be a modest 139 m/456 ft, but it commands a beautiful view of the whole town – and is home to a lot of monkeys. If the jogging trail to the top is not to your taste, try the excellent Thai food at the *Tung-Ka Café* (tel. 076 2115 00 | *Budget*).

SAM SAN TEMPLE
U A3) (*⽥ a3*)
Tien Sang Sung Moo, the goddess of the sea and patron of sailors and fishermen, is venerated in this Chinese temple on *Krabi Road*. The entrance gate with its artistic sculptures, Chinese characters and glowing colours is highly photogenic – and usually outlined against a blue sky. *Admission free*

THAIHUA MUSEUM ●
(U B3) (*⽥ b3*)
Phuket's oldest Chinese school, dating from 1934, has been turned into a museum. Here you can see many historic photos, exhibits and information about the Thai-Chinese history of Phuket Town. The building in Sino-Portuguese style is also worth seeing. *28 Krabi Rd. | Tue–Sun 11am–7pm | admission 200 baht*

TRICKEYE MUSEUM ●
(U C3) (*⽥ c3*)
At this interactive museum, you become part of the show. You can pose in a chef's hat, take a photo of yourself with the Hulk on the toilet or even save your friend from Thailand's biggest waterfall

– the gallery is a house of fun for the whole family. Give yourself time to create humorous, unique and creative photos and don't forget your camera! *Daily 9am–9pm | admission 500 baht | 130/1 Phang Nga Rd.*

WAT SIREY ☀ (119 F6) (⌀ G10)

When you leave the town centre on Sri Suthat Rd. heading east, you are without noticing it on a causeway that leads to the small island of *Ko Sirey*. It is separated from the main island only by the narrow *klong* (canal) of *Tha Jeen*. Here the Buddhist *Wat Sirey* temple with a reclining Buddha 10 m/33 ft long crowns the top of a hill, from which you enjoy a fine view.

FOOD & DRINK

ANNA'S (U B4) (⌀ b4)

Stylish restaurant within historic walls. The Western food is mediocre, but the Thai dishes are authentic. *Daily 7pm–midnight | 13 Rasada Rd. | near the roundabout | tel. 076 21 05 35 | Budget–Moderate*

BLUE ELEPHANT ★ (U B3) (⌀ b3)

This is the name of a chain of outstanding Thai restaurants in Europe and Asia. In the old quarter of Phuket the blue elephant has unpacked its trunk in an imposing townhouse that is more than 100 years old. Royal Thai cuisine at its very best. And in the restaurant's own school of cookery you can put on the chef's hat yourself or try to carve a melon into a work of art. *Daily 11.30am–10.30pm | 96 Krabi Rd. | tel. 076 35 43 55 | www.blue elephant.com/phuket | Expensive*

LE CAFÉ (U B4) (⌀ b4)

This pleasant little bistro-style café serves Western and Thai meals. *Daily from 10am | 64/5 Rasada Centre | Rasada Rd. | Budget*

INSIDER TIP CHINA INN (U B3) (⌀ b3)

Charming restaurant in a lovingly restored Sino-Portuguese townhouse. The Thai food is authentic and delicious. *Mon–Sat | 20 Thalang Rd. | tel. 076 35 62 39 | Budget–Moderate*

INSIDER TIP HOKKIEN NOODLE SOUP (U B3) (⌀ b3)

Every day until late afternoon a tasty noodle soup in traditional Chinese style is served in this basic eatery for less than a pound/around one US dollar. *At the roundabout near the market | Budget*

INSIDER TIP KA JOK SI (U B4) (⌀ b4)

In this somewhat cramped but cosy historic townhouse with antique decorations you can sample excellent Thai cuisine that is good value for money. Later in the evening, when a ladyboy croons some songs and owner Mr Lek dances the tango, the diners sometimes

★ **Jui Tui Temple**
The home of Chinese gods and goddesses → p. 66

★ **Old Phuket Town**
Townhouses built by the rubber and tin magnates await → p. 67

★ **Rang Hill**
From the top of this hill, Phuket Town lies at your feet → p. 68

★ **Blue Elephant**
The Thai meals are as exquisite as the historic house in which they are served → p. 69

MARCO POLO HIGHLIGHTS

get up on their chairs and applaud – or join in the dancing. *Tue–Sat dinner | 26 Takua Pa Rd. | tel. 076 2179 03 | Moderate*

RAYA THAI CUISINE (U B3) (𝄞 b3)

Thai cuisine served in an old villa slightly set back from the main road. The specialities include curries and fish baked in tamarind sauce. The more contemporary spin-off of this restaurant is situated on the main road and is a popular favourite among locals in the evening. *Daily 10.30am–10pm | 48/1 Dibuk Rd. | tel. 076 218155 | Moderate*

THUNG KA CAFÉ ☆ (U A2) (𝄞 b3)

If you've hiked up the Khao Rang hill overlooking Phuket Town, treat yourself at the top to a coffee or something more substantial from this café's wide choice of dishes. Fantastic views. *Daily 10.30am–11pm | Khao Rang | tel. 076 2115 00 | Budget*

SHOPPING

In the centre of Phuket Town one store follows the other along the main shopping streets: *Ranong, Rasada, Yaowaraj south, Montri* and *Tilok Uthit 1 Rd.* The largest department store in the town centre, with a supermarket, is *Robinson* on *Tilok Uthit 1 Rd.,* behind the Ocean Shopping Mall. The second-largest shopping centre on the island, *Central Festival,* lies on the edge of town on the road leading to Patong. In the evenings, Thais flock to the *night market* on *Ong Sim Phai Rd.,* mainly because of the food stalls. The *Limelight Shopping Center,* situated opposite the small park with the dragon statue, is full of small shops and a food court serving cheap and cheerful Thai dishes where you can grab a soup between shops.

BAN BORAN TEXTILES (U B3) (𝄞 b3)

Tasteful clothing and fabrics made of silk and cotton. *Mon–Sat 10.30am–6.30pm | 51 Yaowarat Rd.*

GEMS GALLERY PHUKET
(121 D2) (𝄞 E10)

This well-established jeweller has another three shops in Bangkok, Pattaya and Chiang Mai and is one of the world's largest jewellers. They have an enormous collection of exclusive items and very experienced staff. You can also take a look in the studio. *Daily 9am–6pm |99/35, 888 Moo 5 | Chaloemphrakiat Rama 9 Rd. | north of the centre | www.gems-gallery.com*

LOW BUDGET

The *Thavorn Hotel* will give you a room with a fan for 250 baht, and one with air-conditioning for 500 baht. The rooms are not very modern, but spacious (and those facing the street are noisy). Part of the old-world lobby has been designated a ● museum showing historical photos of Phuket Town. *200 rooms | 74 Rasada Rd. | tel. 076 2113 33*

Delicious authentic Thai food and great value for money: No surprise really that it's hard to get a table for lunch at the *Mee Ton Poe Restaurant.* Since 1946, the restaurant has been serving rice and noodle dishes as well as its speciality – fried Hokkien noodles for between 60 and 150 baht. *Daily 8am–8pm | at the roundabout opposite the clock tower*

NAKA WEEKEND MARKET
(120 C3) (*E11*)

This market is a hive of activity. When the Naka Market opens its gates at the weekend, crowds of locals and tourists swarm in for the enormous selection of produce, cheap prices and delicious food served at the endless stalls and restaurants. You'll find everything your heart desires from

without any chemical additives. *16 Thalang Rd.*

RADSADA HANDMADE
(U B/C4) (*b3*)

Various Buddha statues, beautiful arts and crafts made of coconut or wood as well as a variety of fabrics and smaller pieces of furniture – you may pick up the

The market stands are piled high with tempting exotic fruit and vegetables

exotic fruit, t-shirts, sandals to animals. And if you're not looking for anything, just stroll around taking in the hustle and bustle. *Sat/Sun 4–9pm | approx. 1 km/0.6 mile south of Central Festival on the 4022 towards Rawai*

INSIDER TIP OLDEST HERBS SHOP
(U B3) (*b3*)

This traditional Chinese herbalist was opened in 1917 by the grandfather of the current owner, Mr Wiwan. It still smells of medicinal herbs, as it has for generations. If you describe your ailment, the remedy to cure it will be prepared for you,

perfect souvenir while strolling around. *Daily 9am–8pm | 29 Rasada Rd*

SOUTHWIND BOOKS (U B3) (*b3*)

You won't find a better selection of books and magazines on the whole island. All the books are second-hand, but they are available in many languages, including English of course. *3 Phang Nga Rd.*

THINK POSITIVE (KIT DEE)
(U B3) (*b3*)

The potpourri of goods in this shop can be overwhelming as well as mesmerizing, ranging from Cashmere wool Asian art

Martial art with hands and feet: muay thai, Thai boxing, is the national sport

tapestry, wooden Buddha heads from Burma and Chinese terracotta statues. *Daily 9am–9pm | 15 Yaowarat Rd.*

INSIDER TIP WUA ART GALLERY
(U C3) (*c3*)

Mr Zen is an artist who paints in a minimalist style, and is pleased to have a chat with visitors. He has designed his gallery as a complete work of art in itself. *Daily 10am–10pm | 95 Phang Nga Rd.*

ENTERTAINMENT

While most tourists prefer to look for entertainment in the beach bars, the locals like to go to the nightclubs, pubs, coffee shops and karaoke joints in town. However, there are some places where both Thais and *falang* with local knowledge can be found, for example in the rustic *Timber Hut Pub (118/1 Yaowaraj Rd.)*, where a rock band hottens things up every evening except Sunday from 9pm. In *Rockin Angels (daily 8pm–1am | 54 Yaowaraj Rd. | just before the junction with Thalang Rd.)* Patrick rocks with his musician friends. Resident *falang* meet up in *Michaels Bar (daily 5pm–1am |* *Takua Pa Rd. www.phuket-town.com/michaels)* beneath the big screen or to play pool. Young, hip Thais like to dance at *Kor Tor Mor (daily 8pm–2am | 41/5 Chana Charoen Rd. | near Robinson).* Live bands and DJs with a liking for hip-hop provide the sound.

Films are shown in English on several screens at the *Paradise Multiplex* on *Tilok Uthit Road* next to the Ocean Shopping Centre. Thai boxing is staged every Friday from 8pm in the *boxing stadium (Saphan Hin)* at the south end of Phuket Road, approx. 2 km/1.25 miles outside the centre.

WHERE TO STAY

In terms of value for money, the accommodation here is much better than on the beaches. As the island is not very large, staying in town is an option worth considering, for example to start off while you take a closer look at the beaches.

CRYSTAL INN (U C4) (*c4*)

A modern urban hotel that would cost at least twice as much for the same facilities near a beach. All rooms have air-conditioning, TV, minibar. Central location. *54 rooms | 2/1–10 Soi Surin | Montri Rd. | tel. 076 25 67 89 | www.phuketcrystalinn. com | Budget*

THE MEMORY AT ON ON HOTEL
(U B3) (📖 b3)

This 1920s establishment close to the centre of town is a part of town history: as the most popular backpacker hostel in Phuket Town, it was a film location for The Beach with Leonardo DiCaprio. After a thorough renovation it offers decent double rooms and dorm beds. *49 rooms | 19 Phang Nga Rd. | tel. 076 22 57 40 | www.thememoryhotel.com | Budget*

PEARL HOTEL **(U C4) (📖 c4)**

Once the top address, now showing its age a bit, but it has all necessary amenities and a lovely small pool – as well as live music in the coffee shop in the evenings and an excellent Chinese restaurant on the premises. The massage salon is not an unusual feature in a Thai hotel and causes no annoyance. Central location. *250 rooms | 42 Montri Rd. | tel. 076 36 37 00 | www.pearlhotel.co.th | Moderate*

ROYAL PHUKET CITY **(U D4) (📖 d4)**

The best hotel in town, good value for money. Gym, pool, sauna, spa. For the most delicious cakes in Phuket Town, head for the in-house INSIDER TIP *Bistro 154*. *251 rooms | 154 Phang Nga Rd. | opposite the bus station | tel. 076 23 33 33 | www.royal phuketcity.com | Moderate–Expensive*

THALANG GUESTHOUSE **(U B3) (📖 b3)**

This accommodation occupies a 70-year-old townhouse. The basic rooms come equipped with a fan or air-conditioning. ☆ Two rooms on the top floor have a balcony with a great view of the street, and owner Mr Ti is extremely helpful. *12 rooms | 37 Thalang Rd. | tel. 076 21 42 25 | www.talangguesthouse.com | Budget*

INFORMATION

TOURISM AUTHORITY OF THAILAND
(TAT) (U C3) (📖 c3)

Accommodation listings, transport timetables and brochures, including information from private service providers, are available here. *191 Thalang Rd. | tel. 076 21 10 36 | tatphket@tat.or.th*

WHERE TO GO

BOAT LAGOON (123 D3) (📖 F8)

Landlubbers are welcome in the Boat Lagoon, Phuket's oldest marina, with its restaurants, bars and cafés. Here you can buy or charter a yacht *(Thepkasattri Rd., approx. 10 km/6 miles north of Phuket Town, towards the airport)*. Excellent French cuisine is served at the small restaurant *Le Winch (Mon 11am–2.30pm, Tue–Sat 11am–2.30pm and 6–10pm | tel. 08 48 42 82 28 | Moderate–Expensive)*. The baked goods, cakes and chocolates for sale at the patisserie are delightful.

PHUKET TIN MINING MUSEUM ●
(119 D4) (📖 E9)

Phuket was a prosperous island in days gone by, too. The money lay underground in those days: tin. This interesting museum presents the conditions in which the metal was extracted. There is even a complete reconstruction of a tunnel with life-size miners. The exhibitions tell you all about Phuket's tin-mining history, in a fine building in the Sino-Portuguese architectural style. About 7 km/4.5miles north of Phuket Town in a green environment. *Mon–Sat 9am–4pm | admission 100 baht | on the road that branches off from the highway to the British International School (just after the junction of by-pass 402 with the highway, approx. 1.5 km/1 mile west of the school) | tel. 076 32 21 40*

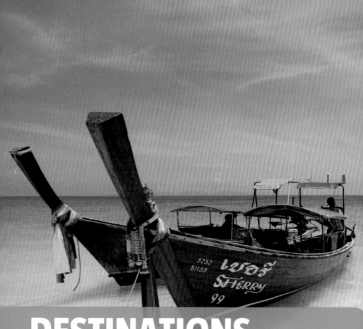

DESTINATIONS AROUND PHUKET

Many islands surround Phuket, like emeralds lying on blue velvet. A few of them have sugar-white beaches, others are merely limestone rocks in strange shapes.

PHANG NGA BAY

(122 B3) (*G–H 1–2*) ★ **Phang Nga Bay** northeast of Phuket is speckled with limestone islands and rocks. On some of the islands there are caves with stalactites and stalagmites, which can only be entered at low tide in a canoe or a longtail boat.

In 1974 a scene for The Man with the Golden Gun was filmed here. In the background is *Ko Tapu,* "Nail Island", which really does look like a nail driven into the sea thanks to the erosion of its rocky base by the waves.

Ko Pannyi is often wrongly marketed under the name *Sea Gypsy Island*. In fact the inhabitants of the houses built on stilts in shallow water at the foot of this huge rocky massif are Muslim families. The restaurants at the edge of the village are an obligatory port of call for all organised tours to Phang Nga. They are included in the programme of every travel agency, and go from Phuket by bus to Phang Nga and the pier of Tha Dan. Here boats await to take visitors through the bay. The journey time from the mainland bridge in the

This is a picture postcard – jungle and fine-grained sand, bizarrely shaped rocks and turquoise water...

north of Phuket is approximately 50 minutes.

Alternatively you can set out on a boat trip directly from Phuket. Boats for Phang Nga Bay depart from the pier of *Ao Po* (117 E5) *(ᶆ G5) (a one-day charter of a longtail costs approx. 4000 baht, spaces for eight passengers).* A particularly romantic way to do the trip is to take the junk *June bahtra (day tour approx. 3700 baht, sunset trip approx. 2500 baht | book through travel agents or at www. asian-oasis.com/june-bahtra-cruise.html).*

The bay with rocks rising steeply from the water looks at its best in the gentle light of the rising sun or in the afternoon. If you would like to undertake the trip independently, you can stay the night below the pier of Tha Dan right by the water (not a swimming beach!) in the comfortable *Phang Nga Bay Resort (88 rooms | 20 Tha Dan Rd. | tel. 076 412067 | Moderate)* and then charter a longtail at the pier. The day trip costs approx. 4500 baht, and eight people fit into the boat.

One of the most popular postcard motifs in Thailand: from the viewpoint on Ko Phi Phi

KO LONE

(120–121 C–D 5–6) (⟡ E–F 13–14) **Al-though it is only 15 minutes from the pier in Chalong, this mountainous jungle island, inhabited only by a few fishermen and rubber tappers, is a natural paradise for those in search of peace and quiet.**

WHERE TO STAY

CRUISER ISLAND RESORT ⊛
Attractive bungalows with air-conditioning and TV. Pool, tennis court. The environmentally aware management promotes recycling and protection of the corals. Booking office in *Rawai (Soi Sermsuk | Viset Rd.), tel. 076 38 32 10). 34 rooms | www.cruiserislandresort.com | Expensive*

KO PHI PHI

(121 E–F 5–6) (⟡ G–H 13–14) **On a list of the world's most beautiful islands, ★ Ko Phi Phi would have a good chance of taking one of the top places.** The island consists of green mountains submerged in the sea, with dramatic rock formations and beaches to die for,

surrounded by waters that are among the best in the world for diving and snorkelling. Paradise has a downside, however. Almost every square metre that could be built on in the island village or Tonsai *(Ban Laem Trong)* has been put to use. Thousands of day trippers, who come on the fleet of ferries from Phuket, Krabi and Lanta, crowd the narrow streets of the centre. Holidaymakers who stay overnight on Ko Phi Phi don't have the island to themselves until the afternoon. They include many young people who like to party – and are not aware that they are staying in a Muslim village. *www.phi-phi.com | www.phiphihotels.info | www.phiphi.phuket.com*

SIGHTSEEING

VIEWPOINT ● ⚲ (121 F6) (⟡ H14)
Behind Tonsai Village it's a half-hour walk up a steep but maintained path to the viewpoint. At the top, ice-cold drinks are served and you can admire one of the most popular postcard views in all Thailand. If you prefer not to go back the same way, you can descend in about 20 minutes through the woods on an extremely steep, unpaved path to INSIDER TIP *Ran Ti Bay* which has a few basic bungalows, as well as longtails that can take you back to the village.

Monkey Beach is also worth a visit – not just to see the furry creatures who give the beach its name but also for the great INSIDER TIP snorkelling opportunities.

FOOD & DRINK

The numerous restaurants in the island's little village serve Thai food and seafood, but also international dishes. The best address is *Le Grand Bleu* (*Moderate*). Good coffee, delicious banana pancakes and more available at ≈ *Aroy Kaffeine* (*Budget*); with fantastic views of the bay at no extra charge.

SPORTS & ACTIVITIES

More than a dozen diving bases compete on Phi Phi. This keeps prices low and offers a good choice to the diving community.

ENTERTAINMENT

In several rustic bars and open-air pubs, partying in the village goes on into the small hours. The trendy place is *Carlitos Bar*. *Hippies Bar* is another favourite haunt for night owls who admire the fire show.

WHERE TO STAY

In the main season – especially around New Year – this island is crowded. Advance booking is essential. And bear in mind that this island is bursting with visitors, which means you don't get the best value for money.

THE BEACHA CLUB
(121 F6) (*𝄞 H14*)
Modern hotel with two houses directly on the beach front. ≈ Large rooftop terrace offering great views. Just a few metres away from the sea and the party mile is also in close vicinity. *42 rooms | tel. 09 37 79 20 10 | www.thebeachaclub. com | Moderate*

PHI PHI ISLAND VILLAGE BEACH
RESORT (121 F5) (*𝄞 H13*)
The prettily furnished bungalows profit from their stunning location in a splen-

---

★ **Phang Nga Bay**
Where limestone rocks rise from the sea → p. 74

★ **Ko Phi Phi**
Film set: twin islands of the kind adored by Hollywood → p. 76

★ **Ko Raya Yai**
A hilly jungle in the sea with superb beaches → p. 79

★ **Ko Similan**
A colourful underwater world in one of the top diving destinations on the planet → p. 79

★ **Ko Yao Noi**
Where hornbills fly – a relaxing green island→ p. 80

MARCO POLO HIGHLIGHTS

did bay with their own private beach – the resort stands alone in the bay and is far away from the lively party scene in the island's village. Excursions are also organised. *156 rooms | tel. 075 62 89 00 | www.phiphi-islandvillage.com | Moderate–Expensive*

KO PHI PHI LE (122 C6) (*Ⓜ j6*)

The small *(le)* uninhabited sister island of Phi Phi Don *(don* meaning large) rises from the deep-blue sea like a castle hewn from rock. It is worth taking a look at the *Viking Cave*. The origin of the rock

A film set and stunning rocky scenery: Maya Bay on Ko Phi Phi Le

WHERE TO GO

Boat tours including a lunch box and snorkelling gear for a fixed price are on offer everywhere. You can charter a longtail for a fixed price. Signs with information and prices at the pier.

INSIDER TIP ▶ KO MAI PAI
(122 C5) (*Ⓜ j5*)

Day trippers seldom set foot on *Bamboo Island*, as Ko Mai Pai is also known, as this flat, tiny island is most suitable for visitors to Phi Phi who have plenty of time. The water and the beach could not be more attractive.

paintings, which are reminiscent of Viking ships, is dubious, but the bamboo poles hanging from the roof of the cave are definitely genuine. Bold collectors of swallows' nests use them to climb up and pluck off the spittle-glued nests of salangan swallows. The crowds of tourists which visit the bay have meant that the cove can only be seen from the outside.

Phi Le Bay is a stunning rocky cove with turquoise-coloured water. *Maya Bay* even surpasses it: walls of limestone rise from the water to heights of up to 200 m/650 ft, forming a breathtaking natural arena. *The Beach* with Leonardo Di-

Caprio was filmed here. Rangers patrol the beach and charge all foreigners 200 baht admission to the national park. It is best to come here in the morning or late afternoon, when things are quieter!

KO RAYA YAI

(122 A6) (*ℳ g6*) ★ **A few fishermen's families, beach bars and eight resorts share this mountainous green island with snowy-white beaches. Although day trippers do visit, you can get the perfect island feeling here.**

And if you want real tranquillity, simply take a 15-minute walk to the other side of the island. Tours to Raya (also spelled Racha) are on offer at every travel agent's. Speedboats make the crossing from Chalong pier in 40 minutes in the morning. They can take up to 20 passengers *(return trip approx. 1500 baht)*.

WHERE TO STAY

BUNGALOW RAYA RESORT ❧
Plain bungalows with shower and fan (the power goes off at midnight) on a slope with a fantastic view. What could be nicer than enjoying the sea view from your own balcony? The resort also has a good restaurant right by the sea. *20 rooms | tel. 076 35 20 87 | www.bunga lowraya.com | Moderate*

THE RACHA ☺
This stunningly beautiful resort on a wonderful white beach offers environmentally sound accommodation in villas. As few trees as possible were felled to build it – and for every one that was chopped down, two new trees were planted. Palms are allowed to grow through the roofs wherever possible. Most waste is recycled, and the beach is cleaned daily.

Guests at the resort have to share it with daytrippers, however. Two pools, tennis court, gym and spa. *85 rooms | office in Chalong close to the pier | tel. 076 35 54 55 | www.theracha.com | Expensive*

KO SIMILAN

(0) (*ℳ 0*) ★ **These nine jungle-covered rocky islands 110 km/70 miles northwest of Phuket are uninhabited and have only a few small sandy beaches.**

It is what lies underwater that makes them so fascinating. The Similans are among the world's top diving destinations. At visibility of up to 30 m/100 ft, divers and snorkellers have the chance to see big fish such as whale sharks and mantas as well as a sensational display of corals. All the diving stations offer trips to the Similans lasting several days on motor yachts or sailing yachts. Travel agencies also run day trips for snorkel-

LOW BUDGET

Although the furnishing and service is extremely basic, ❧ some of the Bamboo Bungalow huts have fantastic views and cling to the hillside in the west of Ao Lo Dalam and cost around 1000 baht. *12 rooms | tel. 08 97 25 48 84*

Rooms for 1000 baht right on the beach? *Baan Tha Khao Bungalows (6 rooms | tel. 076 58 27 33 | www.ko hyaobungalow.com)* on Ko Yao Noi fit the bill. And for 500 baht per day you can rent a kayak.

lers and tours including an overnight stay on island no. 4. Minibuses depart from Phuket for Taplamu on the mainland (approx. two hours). From there, the crossing by speedboat to Similan takes about 1.5 hours. The islands are a 🌐 national park *(admission 200 baht)*, and the park authority makes accommodation in bungalows or tents available for overnight guests *(www.dnp.go.th)*. During the monsoon season from early May until late October the park is closed.

KO YAO NOI

(122 B4) (∅ h4) The second-largest island in the bay of Phang Nga is a green gem in the sea that can be reached by ferry from Phuket in half an hour – yet few tourists find their way here. The reason is that ⭐ Ko Yao Noi has no wonderful beaches, and the water recedes a long way at low tide.

But this is a blessing! The island, populated by 4000 Muslim farmers and fishermen, has retained its authentic charm. It is a perfect spot for relaxing and enjoying the natural surroundings. Ferries go several times daily from Phuket (Bang Rong pier on the east coast) and from Krabi Province (Thalane pier). *www.koh-yao-islands.com | www.kohyaotravel.com*

FOOD & DRINK

In the island's main settlement, which is simply named *Talad* (market), Dora from Denmark and Stephane from France serve not only vegan and vegetarian fare but also real Thai coffee and cocktails in their likeable INSIDER TIP ▶ *Faye's Restaurant (daily 9am–9pm | tel. 076 59 74 95 | Budget–Moderate)*. On the ring road just before Pasai Beach *Rice Paddy* dishes up steak and sautéed potatoes *(tel. 076*

45 42 55 | Budget–Moderate). Also on the ring road, just before Takhao Bay, at *La Luna (tel. 08 46 29 15 50 | www.lalunakohyao.com | Budget–Moderate)*, the pizza comes fresh from the oven. At *Pasai Seafood (tel. 08 72 64 12 81 | Budget–Moderate)* on the beach of the same name you can enjoy Thai meals and seafood right on the beach.

SHOPPING

Small shops on the beaches and the ring road sell essential items. The main village has a few shops catering to daily needs and the island's only air-conditioned *7-Eleven* shop, but it sells no alcohol. However, there is a cash machine at 7-Eleven. The *Wine Shop* next to *Faye's Restaurant* stocks a selection of wines and spirits.

SPORTS & ACTIVITIES

Many resorts and tour operators hire out kayaks and organise tours to the islands in the bay of Phang Nga. You can also hire a bike and set off on the good, quiet island ring road, to explore a large part of Ko Yao Noi in about 1.5 hours (see tour on p. 94). Look into the green jungle treetops: The island is home to many birds, and even the rare hornbill can be seen here.

IK.Y.N BOXCAMP

Fists fly at this box camp run by the former Thai champion Khun Hlukhin and his experienced team of trainers. Accommodation is provided in a former hotel now home to Thai boxing students. *Courses available all year round; you can begin any day, but there is a limited number of students | Lamsai | tel. 08 22 89 42 76 | www.phuket-krabi-muaythai.com*

ISLAND YOGA ●

Yoga retreats in the green outdoors surrounded by stunning scenery. You stay a minimum of three nights but many spend a week to immerse themselves fully in the intense yoga experience. Also suitable for beginners. *You can begin on any day, closed between May and September | Klong Jark Beach | at Ulmar's Nature Lodge | Tel. 08 73 87 94 75 | thailandyogaretreats.com*

INSIDER TIP MINA'S COOKING CLASSES

Would you like to perfect your Thai cooking skills? In small groups, you learn to cook five amazing dishes and can take the recipe book home with you – a great souvenir for you to treasure. Children's cookery courses are also organised. A shuttle service from the bungalow is included in the price. *Daily 10.30am–3pm and 15.30–6pm | Ban Yai | tel. 08 78 77 31 61 | www.minas-cooking-classes.com*

WHERE TO STAY

Almost all accommodation runs along the beaches of the east coast, which are accessed via the ring road. About two dozens resorts, most of them basic, cater for guests. *Six Senses,* by contrast, is an absolutely top-class haven, one of the most exclusive resorts in southern Thailand.

KOYAO ISLAND RESORT ◉

Koyao Island Resort is an extremely exclusive eco resort so there is no air-conditioning or TVs in the rooms. The traditionally furnished villas (up to 120 m^2) are designed exclusively with natural materials which do not store heat, promote air circulation and blend perfectly into the palm forest directly at the seafront. *22 rooms | Klong Jark Beach | tel. 076 59 74 74 | www.koyao.com | Expensive*

SABAI CORNER

The veteran amongst the resorts on Koy Yao is beautifully located beneath trees

Water buffalos on Ko Yao Noi: the island for nature lovers and those in search of tranquillity

Pool with palms and private beach: eco-luxury at the Six Senses

on a slope next to the sea. Wooden bungalows with fans, roofed with palm fronds, of various sizes: you can rent a house sleeping five. Cosy restaurant. *11 rooms | Klong Jark Beach | tel. 076 59 74 97 | www.sabaicornerbungalows. com | Budget–Moderate*

SIX SENSES ✪

In this upmarket resort, the villas are mainly built from natural materials, and the bedrooms are air-conditioned. The grounds slope down from a jungle-covered hill to a small private beach. Guests can explore the mangrove forest next door on boardwalks. Fruit and vegetables are grown in the resort's own garden, waste is composted, and no plastic bottles are used here. Pool, spa, gym, tennis court. *50 rooms | between Klong Jark Beach and Takhao Bay | tel. 076 41 85 00 | www.six senses.com/sixsensesyaonoi | Expensive*

INSIDER TIP SUNTISOOK RESORT

A family-run business, where guests feel at home. Manager Chui looks after everything and cooks with her mother – mashed potatoes too! Spacious bungalows with air-conditioning, TV, refrigerator or fan in a well-kept garden. You cross a very quiet road to get to the beach. *9 rooms | Takhao Bay | tel. 076 58 27 50 | Budget–Moderate*

KO YAO YAI

(122 B4–5) (*ꔛ h4–5*) **The larger of the two Yao islands is twice as big and twice as long (approx. 25 km/15 miles) as its little sister. Tourism is not even in its infancy here – it is just being born.**
Outside the few resorts there is hardly any tourist infrastructure on this island with its seven villages. It is just right for nature lovers in search of tranquillity who would like to experience authentic, rural island life. Most of the 12,000 in-

habitants live in the south of the island, which can be reached daily by ferry from Phuket harbour or the Bang Rong pier. The boats to Ko Yao Noi stop at the north of the island on the way. *www.koh-yao-islands.com | www.koyaotravel.com*

FOOD & DRINK

At the Loh Jark pier in the south of the island you can eat grilled chicken and spicy papaya salad at cooked-food stalls with a sea view. On the access road to the pier, the *Bua Siam restaurant (Budget)* even lists its Thai dishes on an English-language menu.

SHOPPING

A concrete road runs the length of the island from north to south. Scattered along it are small shops that sell food and everyday items. Most of the shops are to be found in the south at the main settlement by the pier.

SPORTS & ACTIVITIES

The main road, which has very little traffic, and the tracks that branch off it to the beaches are ideal for mountain-bikers. Most of the resorts hire out bikes and mopeds. Mr Virote, manager of the *Activities Resort (main road in the south of the island | tel. 076 58 24 75 | www.kohyaoactivitiesresort.com)* not only has bungalows, but also runs ⚙ ecological tours, e.g. INSIDER TIP kayak trips through the mangroves at full moon, as well as horse-riding through the forests and countryside, and to the beaches. *Elixir Divers (in the Elixir Resort | tel. 08 78 97 00 76 | www.elixirdivers.com)* is the island's only diving base.

WHERE TO STAY

ELIXIR RESORT

Luxurious bungalows roofed with palm straw in an extensive garden right by the beach. This is the best accommodation at the south end of the island. With pool and gym. *31 rooms | Loh Yark Bay | tel. 08 78 08 38 38 | www.elixirresort.com | Expensive*

INSIDER TIP HEIMAT GARDENS

Yamalia brings a touch of the Alps to Thailand: she was born on Ko Yao Yai, but lived in the part of German-speaking Tyrol that belongs to Italy. The clean rooms with air-conditioning, TV, refrigerator and balcony in a terraced house are good value for money. It is a five-minute walk to the almost deserted beach of Lo Paret. Yamalia also organises tours. *5 rooms | south of the island | turn-off from the main road to Lo Paret Beach | tel. 08 57 94 74 28 | www.heimatgardens.com | Budget*

KO YAO YAI VILLAGE ⚙

Surrounded by rubber trees and rainforest, the bungalows have a roof of palm straw and a canopy of leaves above. A natural environment, but no need to forego creature comforts. Vegetables are grown in the garden. Gym, spa with sauna, big pool with a fantastic view of Phang Nga Bay. At low tide the sea goes out a long way, and the beach is rocky. *49 rooms | north of the island | tel. 076 58 45 00 | www.kohyaoyaivillage.com | Expensive*

YAO YAI BEACH RESORT

Bungalows on stilts in a garden right by the sea, with cladding of bamboo mats and a thatched roof, with air-conditioning or fan. All have TV and refrigerator. *19 rooms | Lo Paret Beach | south of the island | tel. 08 19 68 46 41 | www.yaoyairesort.com | Budget–Moderate*

DISCOVERY TOURS

① PHUKET AT A GLANCE

START: ① Ao Chalong **END:** ⑩ Patong Beach	1 day Driving time (without stops) 2 ½ hours
Distance: ➡ 94 km/58 miles	

COSTS: Approx. 3,100 baht for car hire, petrol, admission fees, food and drink

WHAT TO PACK: swimwear, sun cream

IMPORTANT TIPS: Drive with extreme caution in Phuket due to the high number of accidents!

Magnificent beaches and a capital city with flair, history and nature, practising Buddhism and excessive consumerism – in one action-packed day, you can see more of Phuket than many visitors manage during their entire holiday.

Would you like to explore the places that are unique to this region? Then the Discovery Tours are just the thing for you – they include terrific tips for stops worth making, breathtaking places to visit, selected restaurants and fun activities. It's even easier with the Touring App: download the tour with map and route to your smartphone using the QR Code on pages 2/3 or from the website address in the footer below – and you'll never get lost again even when you're offline.

→ p. 2/3

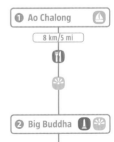

10:00am Start your trip where others anchor their boats. The bay of ❶ **Ao Chalong** → p. 58 is a natural harbour for yachts and a meeting place for sailors from all over the world. While enjoying a hearty farmer's breakfast in **Dickies Lighthouse Restaurant and Bar** → p. 60 at the end of the road to the left of the pier, you have a panoramic view of the bay and all the boats. **After that drive from the pier to the roundabout and take the second road on the right in the direction of the airport. After approx. 1 km/half a mile, a turn-off to the** ❷ **Big Buddha** → p. 59 is signposted on

❶ Ao Chalong

8 km/5 mi

❷ Big Buddha

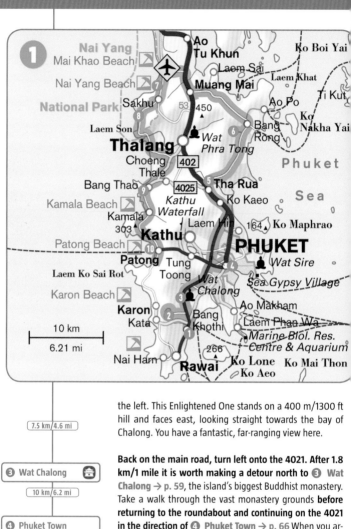

the left. This Enlightened One stands on a 400 m/1300 ft hill and faces east, looking straight towards the bay of Chalong. You have a fantastic, far-ranging view here.

Back on the main road, turn left onto the 4021. After 1.8 km/1 mile it is worth making a detour north to ❸ Wat Chalong → p. 59, the island's biggest Buddhist monastery. Take a walk through the vast monastery grounds **before returning to the roundabout and continuing on the 4021 in the direction of ❹ Phuket Town → p. 66** When you arrive, you can shop and stroll in Thalang Road and its side street Soi Rommani in the historic quarter. A lot of old houses with shops in the Sino-Portuguese style make this district attractive. Head to **China Inn → p. 69**, where you will be served a drink in this beautifully restored townhouse.

Take Highway 402 towards the airport as far as the Heroines Monument → p. 36, then turn right onto road no.

7.5 km/4.6 mi

❸ Wat Chalong

10 km/6.2 mi

❹ Phuket Town

16 km/10 mi

4027 (if the roundabout is closed, continue straight on and then take a 180-degrees turn) to ⑤ **Thalang National Museum** → p. 36. Here you can learn all about the history of Phuket. **Continue on the 4027 heading north, and after approx. 7 km/4.3 miles turn left into the jungle** of the ⑥ **Khao Phra Thaeo National Park** → p. 36 (signposted). The **Gibbon Rehabilitation Centre** explains how these primates are prepared for a life in the wild.

⑤ **Thalang National Museum** 🏛
10 km/6.2 mi
⑥ **Khao Phra Thaeo National Park**
23 km/14 mi

`01:00pm` **Back on the highway going north, cross the green inland of Phuket via Bang Rong village, turn right after around 2 km/1.2 mile onto the 402. At the next opportunity, take a 180-degree turn towards the airport and follow the sign on the left to** ⑦ **Nai Yang Beach** → p. 47. How about a quick dip in the sea before treating yourself to some freshly barbecued fish at **Khwanta-Seafood** (daily 8am–8pm | Moderate) on the beach road? After lunch **follow the road south to** ⑧ **Nai Thon Beach** → p. 46, a top beach address. Enjoy a relaxing stroll by the sea followed by a massage on the beach afterwards. If you like things even quieter, **park approx. 2 km/1.2 mile south of Nai Thon by the side of the road above the bay of** Hin Kruai → p. 47. Look out for the signpost to "Banana Beach". A little path leads down to this sandy beach.

A cuddly gibbon

The coastal road now takes you inland again. Drive along road no. 4030 and then 4025, always heading south as far as ⑨ **Surin Beach** → p. 56, which has been ecologically restored and is today one of the island's prettiest beaches. The inland road offers some good restaurants.

`06:00pm` When the sun goes down, make your way to ⑩ **Patong Beach** → p. 49 **13 km/8 miles south of Surin. Simply follow the coastal road.** The touristic heart of Phuket is one big show – and you have to have seen it. Stroll through the zone of bars on the Bangla Road and drink a beer in the long-established **Kangaroo Bar**. Affordable and tasty food in the evening is available at **Pum Restaurant** → p. 52. If you still have enough energy for a shopping spree, then go to **Jungceylon** → p. 52 the island's largest shopping centre. Simply follow the Bangla Road from the beach to the end and then keep right. You can shop here to your heart's content until 11pm.

17 km
⑦ **Nai Yang Beach** 🔁 🧺 🍴
8.5 km/5.3 mi
⑧ **Nai Thon Beach** 🔁 🧍 Ⓟ
17 km/10.5 mi
🔁
⑨ **Surin Beach** 🔁 🍴
14 km/8.7 mi
⑩ **Patong Beach** 🍹 🍴 🛍

2 WALKING WITH A VIEW

START: ❶ Nai Harn Beach	1 day
END: ❶ Nai Harn Beach	Walking time
	(without stops)
Distance:	Difficulty:	approx. 4 hours
🕐 12 km/7.5 mi	ıl easy	

COSTS: approx. 775 baht for food, drink sauna and massage
WHAT TO PACK: sun cream, swimwear and snorkelling gear, water, comfortable walking shoes

IMPORTANT TIPS: Drink plenty of water when you are walking and do not forget to wear a hat.

In the most scenic part of the island, deep in the south, there is a route on which you can walk more or less undisturbed from one beach to another with spectacular views and wonderful spots for relaxing, swimming, snorkelling and even a massage on the way.

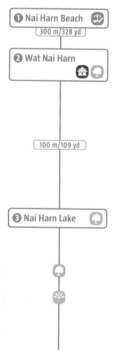

❶ Nai Harn Beach
300 m/328 yd

❷ Wat Nai Harn

100 m/109 yd

❸ Nai Harn Lake

08:00am The excursion starts with a visit to the monastery. On the approach road to ❶ **Nai Harn Beach → p. 62 you will see a large car park on the left** just before you reach the beach. From here you can enter ❷ **Wat Nai Harn**. When you stroll through the monastery grounds, look out for a huge INSIDER TIP banyan tree just to the left of the path which is decorated with an odd collection of little shrines, dried garlands of flowers, dolls, miniature elephants and Buddhist statues – a "ghost cemetery" for ancient altar figures. The elaborately decorated central temple building with its glass mosaics glittering in the sun is also worth looking at.

You can't miss the **path to the back gate of the monastery.** When you have passed **through the gate,** a promenade lined by trees leads around ❸ **Nai Harn Lake** in front of you. **Bear right and continue by the lake** until you reach a small Chinese shrine. **Take the right fork up towards Cape Promthep.** This is a quiet road, with woodland to the left and right. The road ascends in curves until, high above the sea, you get a glimpse of Nai Harn Beach through the vegetation and a bird's eye view of the lake there.

But the best view is yet to come! When the wind generator of the ④ **Promthep Alternative Energy Station** → p. 64 appears in front of you, **take the path that branches off to the right,** and after only a few paces you will see a viewing platform high above the sea. The panorama of the bay, flanked by green hills with an uninhabited island in the middle, is stunning. **Back on the road,** you now descend to sea level. The tiny beach of ⑤ **Ya Nui Beach** → p. 65 is a good place for a swim, and if you have your snorkel and mask with you, take the opportunity to admire the corals and fish under water.

01:00pm From Ya Nui a road **goes off left** towards Rawai. Here too there is little traffic, but lots of greenery to the left and right. **After about 1.5 km/1 mile you will reach the road that rises from Rawai to Cape Promthep. Bear left here and then right across the bridge.** You can walk along ⑥ **Rawai Beach** → p. 64 on the promenade. A whole row of restaurants along the road serve seafood. Stop for a snack and an iced coffee in **Nikita's Café** *(daily 10am until late | at the end of the beach where the promenade turns inland | Moderate).*

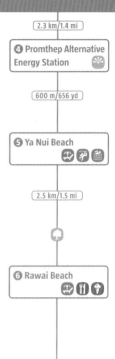

2.3 km/1.4 mi

④ Promthep Alternative Energy Station

600 m/656 yd

⑤ Ya Nui Beach

2.5 km/1.5 mi

⑥ Rawai Beach

Apprentice fisherman on Rawai Beach

4.2 km/2.6 mi

❼ Herbal Steam Sauna

30 m/98 ft

❽ A Spoonful of Sugar

2.1 km/1.3 mi

❶ Nai Harn Beach

From Rawai return to the bridge and cross it, then **follow the road that branches off right.** It will take you past rubber plantations, as well as a lot of resorts, restaurants and houses. After approx. 2 km/1.25 miles it reaches the road to Sai Yuan. **Follow it to the right** and a special treat lies in store. At first the traffic is noticeably heavier, but your reward awaits you **as soon as you pass the 7-Eleven on the right.** Opposite you will see a sign marked **❼ Herbal Steam Sauna** *(daily noon–7pm / sauna 100 baht, massage 300 baht)* for relaxing moments. The facilities here are basic but one of the few which does not have scantily dressed employees dancing around. After a sauna and massage, you can enjoy a coffee and delicious cake in the charming café **❽ A Spoonful of Sugar → p. 62** on the other side of the road.

06:00pm On the way back you can avoid the traffic by **taking the road that goes off to the right opposite the German Bakery → p. 62.** You will then walk in a big loop through green scenery, past resorts and private residences, until you reach **❶ Nai Harn Beach → p. 62** once again.

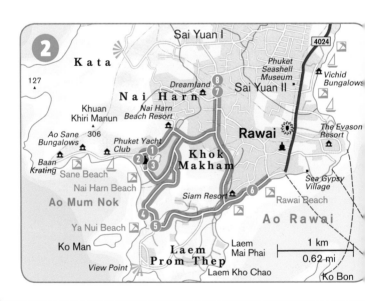

TO THE SOUTH OF THAILAND

START: ❶ Thepkrasattri Bridge END: ❶ Thepkrasattri Bridge	**4 days** Driving time (without stops) approx. 6 hours
Distance: 🚗 approximately 300 km/186 miles	

COSTS: 11,700–15,500 baht (accommodation, food and drink, car hire, petrol)

WHAT TO PACK: swimwear, hiking boots, sun cream, mosquito protection (sprays, long-sleeved t-shirt, socks)

IMPORTANT TIPS: Alcohol and dogs are banned in the Muslim fishing village ❹ Ko Pannyi. There is a risk of leeches and mosquitoes especially evenings and after rainfall in the ❺ Khao Sok National Park.

This route for travellers keen to discover the mainland passes through the loveliest scenery in southern Thailand. You will explore by boat the wonderful world of islands in the bay of Phang Nga, drive a hire car on well-paved roads through lonely jungle areas and walk on long beaches.

Highway 402 leads over ❶ Thepkrasattri Bridge to the mainland and meets in Khok Kloi Highway 4 which you take in the direction of Phang Nga. 30 km/20 mi past Khok Kloi a little road veers off left to the beautifully situated monastery ❷ Wat Suwan Khuha and the cave of INSIDER TIP Tham Yai where you can discover many Buddha statues. **Return to the highway, and turn off right 3 km/2 mi before you reach Phang Nga Town to get to the pier of ❸ Tha Dan and Phang Nga Bay Resort → p. 75.** From here you can explore by boat the wonderful **Phang Nga Bay → p. 74** with mangrove jungle, limestone mountains and caves at your own pace. You can get a basic lunch in one of the no-thrills restaurants.

If you think the scenery of mountains in the sea looks like a film set, you are right: The Man with the Golden Gun was filmed here. Hunting the villain, Roger Moore as James Bond zoomed across the water and even gave his name to a rocky islet *(James Bond Island)*.

You can charter a longtail boat at the pier from one of the boat people *(approx. 4000 baht a day)*. The journey

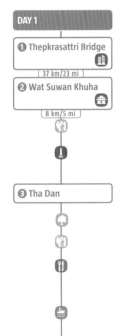

DAY 1

❶ Thepkrasattri Bridge

37 km/23 mi

❷ Wat Suwan Khuha

8 km/5 mi

❸ Tha Dan

30 km/19 mi

④ Ko Pannyi 🛏

through the bay takes between 4 and 6 hours depending on the route recommended by your boater. Accommodation is available in **④ Ko Pannyi,** a Muslim village built on piles, in the basic but pleasant INSIDER TIP *Sayan Bungalows (8 rooms | Budget)* run by the Yaowapa family. Contact and booking at: Mr. Kean Tour *(Phang Nga bus terminal | 111 Phet Kasem Rd. | tel. 0 76 41 11 50)*. Mr. Kean Tour is also a good contact if you want to book a boat in advance instead of turning up at the harbour spontaneously: not everyone likes bartering with the private boat guides.

Boat tour at the Khao Sok National Park

After a good night's sleep, you can organise for a longtail boat to pick you up (ask at your accommodation) and then continue your journey on Highway 4. **At Bang Ba, road no. 4090 branches off left towards Takua Pa. After 50 km/30 miles** through wild, impressive mountain and jungle scenery **east of Takua Pa you reach Highway 401 in the direction of Surat Thani.** After 15 minutes on this road, you will see the sign of ★ **⑤ Khao Sok National Park** *(www. khaosok.com)* on the left. At 646 km²/250 sq. miles, this park is the largest area of jungle in the south of Thailand. Tigers and wild elephants are said to roam the rainforest still and gibbons sometimes put in an appearance near the overnight accommodation. You can even spot the world's biggest flower here, the blossom of the *Rafflesia* can reach a diameter of up to 1 m/3 ft.

DAY 2

95 km/59 mi

⑤ Khao Sok National Park 🐘🛏

Treat yourself to two nights in the park so that you have a whole day for tours. Sleep in one of the bungalows and tree houses at **Our Jungle House** *(20 rooms | tel. 08 14 17 05 46 | www.khaosokaccommodation.com | Budget–Moderate)*.

DAY 3

Amazing natural beauty in the National Park: The resort organises canoe tours and jungle trekking. A fun way to travel by water is INSIDER TIP *tubing* – a leisurely float down the Sok River in a truck tyre. The walking trails close to the park headquarters are well signposted, and guides show you the way through the dense vegetation

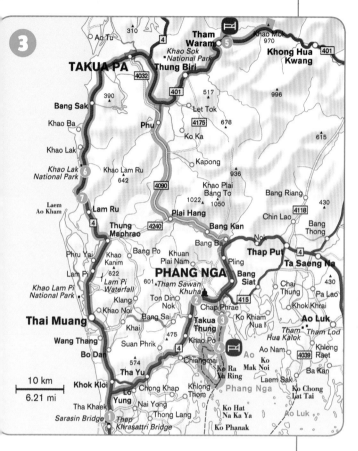

on longer tours. It is definitely worthwhile making a trip to the reservoir of **Cheow Larn**.

On the way back to Phuket (approx. two hours driving time), **south of the provincial town of Takua Pa, Highway 4 takes you** past the endless beaches of ⑥ **Khao Lak**. Many resorts and hotels welcome guests here *(www. khaolak.com)*. For a lovely view of the sea and jungle-covered mountains, go to no-name restaurant at the headquarters of the ⑦ **Khao Lak Lamru National Park** *(daily | Budget)*, 100 m/320 ft right on the highway which winds up a hill here at the southern end of the beach.

DAY 4

[113 km/70 mi]

⑥ Khao Lak

6 km/3.7 mi

⑦ Khao Lak Lamru
National Park

| 52 km/32mi |

① Thepkrasattri Bridge

From this point you head south back to Phuket which you reach over the ① **Thepkrasattri Bridge**.

4 CYCLING AROUND THE ISLAND

START: ① Takhao Pier	1 day
END: ① Takhao Pier	Cycling time
	(without stops)
Distance:	2½–3 hours
🚴 approx. 20 km/12.5 miles	

COSTS: approx. 780 baht for bike hire and food and drink
WHAT TO PACK: swimwear, sunscreen, water

IMPORTANT TIPS: Always wear a hat as well as sun cream on your arms and legs.
You can hire bicycles for example in Suntisook Resort → p. 82 in Takhao Bay.

The thinly populated island of Ko Yao Noi with its good, quiet ring road and tracks is a paradise for cyclists. You'll have fun swimming, paddling and enjoying good food while taking in fantastic views of the sea and jungle.

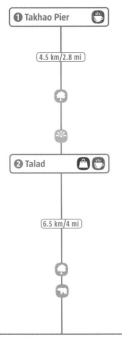

① Takhao Pier

| 4.5 km/2.8 mi |

② Talad

| 6.5 km/4 mi |

10:00am On ① **Takhao Pier** you can sit right by the water enjoying a cup of coffee in the morning peace before you pedal off. **Start by passing through the small village heading inland** and above all upwards because you'll quickly realise that this is a mountainous island. But if you have to go slowly for a few hundred metres, you will enjoy the view of green valleys and hills, jungle and rubber plantations all the more.

From the highest point on the road, a long straight stretch descends again to the main settlement on the island, ② **Talad**. Here you can leave your bike and **take a stroll along the main street with its little shops.** From Faye's Restaurant → p. 80 at the crossroads in the heart of Talad you can watch the easy pace of life here while cooling off with a drink. **Then continue, passing the post office, police station and school heading southeast.** It is not long before you are in green countryside. Here and there you pass a house or shop. In some places you also pedal through mangrove forests close to the coast. Don't be alarmed if a monitor lizard or a snake crosses the road in front of you.

DISCOVERY TOURS

01:00pm In the far south of the island, a dead-end road branches off from the circular road towards Lam Sai. Pass the Lam Sai Village Hotel and continue cycling along the coast until the concrete road turns into a track and then ends. At the water's edge is the restaurant ❸ INSIDER TIP Lam Sai Seafood *(daily 10am–10pm | Budget)*, still known by some and signposted with its former name *Lobster Sea Food* where you can enjoy excellent sea food. You should be back on the **ring road** at 2.30pm at the latest; **where you head right and after a short distance go right again onto a track.** This leads to the ❹ **Lom Lae Beach Resort** *(www.lomlae.com)* ato a lovely beach where you can swim even at low tide (depending on the season and moon phase).

The circular road takes you on to ❺ **Pasai Beach** where several resorts, shops, restaurants and food stalls serve snacks and meals right on the beach. If your legs are getting tired by now, you can have a massage on the beach. And if it's time to exercise your arms, then hire a kayak to paddle up and down the shore.

06:00pm The bike tour now leads **along the east coast,** accompanied by a sea view all the while. The recommendation for the next stop is the pleasant restaurant in the ❻ **Sabai Corner → p. 82**, resort, where the menu lists such exotic combinations as potato salad with tuna. On the return stretch to Takhao Bay there is only one more ascent to manage. **The climb through the forest is over after approx.100 m/100 yds., and then you can freewheel all the way down to** ❼ **La Luna → p. 80**, where you will be rewarded with the cappuccino or espresso that you so richly deserve. **A little further on you pass through a rubber plantation,** where the shining sea is already visible straight ahead. To round off the trip, how about a walk along the beach looking for shells? And if the tide is out, you can even get to a little rocky island of Koh Nok on foot. The tour ends where it started at ❶ **Takhao Pier**.

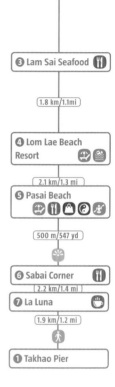

95

SPORTS & ACTIVITIES

If you want to do sports on holiday, you've come to the right place. On Phuket you can dive with whale sharks, go water-skiing or paddle a canoe through a world of wonderful islands.

Most of the operators named below organise numerous and varied tours. Make your booking via the websites or through travel agents on the spot.

CANOE TOURS

The bay of Phang Nga east of Phuket is a wonderful area for canoeing. Among the highlights are caves *(hong)* into which you can paddle at low tide. Canoe tours on the tidal rivers and in the mangrove forests of Krabi Province east of Phuket or on the reservoir in the Khao Sok National Park are also delightful. *Paddle Asia (www.paddleasia.com) | Sea Canoe Thailand (www.seacanoe.net) | Sea Cave Canoe (www.seacavecanoe.com)*.

CLIMBING

The limestone cliffs of the islands in the bay of *Phang Nga* and on *Ko Phi Phi* are a delight for climbers. A day's course costs approx. 1,900 baht. On *Ko Yao Noi* courses are run by *Ko Yao Rock Climbing (www.themountainshop.org)*, on *Phi Phi* by several smaller providers.

DIVING

The Andaman Sea around Phuket is among the best diving areas in the

Deep in the jungle, below the waves
or at the kitchen stove – Phuket is
paradise for active holidays

whole world, although global warming is leading to bleached corals ariund here, too. With visibility of up to 30 m/100 ft you can watch enormous (and harmless) whale sharks or kaleidoscope swarms of coral fish. The uninhabited *Similan* Islands north of Phuket are a highlight. Less well known, but also excellent for divers, are the waters around INSIDER TIP *Ko Surin* north of Similan. Near the underwater reef of *Richelieu Rock* the chances of seeing whale sharks and rays are very good.

The INSIDER TIP coral-covered underwater *Burma Banks* 165 km/100 miles northwest of the Similan Islands are alrready in Burmese waters. This is where experienced divers can make genuinely new discoveries, and see many reef sharks and sharks of the high seas. Only one hour by boat from Phuket, around the Phi Phi Islands, and further south in the archipelago that extends down to the Malaysian border, a rich variety of underwater fauna and flora awaits.

The best season for diving, with calm waters, is January to April. A day trip including two dives costs approx. 2600 baht, a four-day diving trip to Similan or Surin approx. 22,600 baht. For a diving course of three to four days, expect to pay around 11,300 baht. You will find diving schools on Phuket, Phi Phi and both of the Yao Islands. On Ko Phi Phi in particular there is one diving shop next to another. The competition is keen, which keeps prices down. Links to diving schools and tour operators can be found on the website of the state tourist organisation: *www.tourismthailand.org*.

GOLF

Seven golf courses make Phuket the top destination in Thailand for international golf tourism. Green fees start at approx. 2600 baht. The cheapest place to play a round is the INSIDER TIP nine-hole *Phunaka Golf Course (from approx. 950 baht | www.phunakagolf.com)* near Chalong – and it is even open at night, with the course illuminated by floodlights. At the time of going to print, it was still not clear how long the renovation work would last. Arrangements for reduced green fees can be booked through: *Golf Orient (www.golforient.com)* | *Phuket Golf (www.phuket-golf.com)* | *Phuket Golf Master (www.phuketgolf.net)*.

JUNGLE TOURS

Only one patch of rainforest remains on Phuket: the *Kao Phra Kaeo National Park* in the northeast. Two hours by car to the northeast of Phuket, however, in the *Khao Sok National Park (www.khaosok.com)*, tigers and wild elephants still occupy a huge area of jungle. A tour on foot or by kayak through the jungle is an unforgettable experience. Operators: *Phuket Tours (www.phuket-travel.com)* | *Phuket Safari (www.phuket-safari-travel.com)* | *Siam Safari (www.siamsafari.com)*. You can also organise a trip to this national park independently without difficulties, getting there by hire car or on a public bus from Phuket Town.

MOUNTAIN BIKING

You can book half-day tours to explore the south and northeast of the island on tracks and the quieter roads. For a day tour, take a ferry over to *Ko Yao Noi* (see p. 94). Here more and more resorts hire out mountain bikes to their guests. Tours lasting two days often go east to the neighbouring provinces *Phang Nga* and *Krabi*. Tours can be booked through travel agents or directly with the organisers: *Action Holidays Phuket (www.biketoursthailand.com)* | *Siam Bike Tours (www.siambiketours.com)*. *Sea Canoe Thailand (www.seacanoe.net)* also runs mountain bike tours.

SAILING

The islands of the ● Andaman Sea are heaven for sailors, and Phuket with its big marinas is the sailing centre of Asia. You can charter a yacht from several different companies. The costs for a day's charter without a skipper start at around 13,200 euros. Some yacht owners will take paying passengers on the long voyage to Europe or on a trip to the islands between Phuket and Langkawi in Malaysia. They post their offers on the notice boards and walls of restaurants. You have INSIDER TIP the best opportunities of contacting yachtsmen in the bay of Chalong and on Nai Harn

Underwater world in the Andaman Sea: one of the best diving places on the planet

Beach/Ao Sane. This is where most of the private sailing boats that come to Phuket put down anchor. Many leading boat charter companies are represented in the marinas on the east coast of Phuket, for example *Asia Marine Leisure (Boat Lagoon | www.asia-marine. net)*, or *Phuket Yachtcharter (Yacht Haven Marina | www.phuket-yachts. com)*.

SPAS

The ultimate in relaxation and complete rejuvenation: a few hours in a spa are the perfect cure for the body and soul. Herbal baths, steam saunas, wraps and famous Thai massages are not just a remedy for relaxation but for your health too. Further information on the spa resorts and treatments can be found at *www.phuket.com/spa_ massage*.

SWIMMING & SNORKELLING

On Phuket as on all beaches in the south of Thailand, bear in mind that swimming can be dangerous in the rainy season between May and September. When red flags fly on the beaches, take them seriously. Every year tourists are carried out to sea by treacherous currents and drown. If you are swept away by a rip current, do not try to swim against it in panic (you will be completely exhausted after a couple of minutes), but try to swim out of it to the side. On Phuket snorkellers can still find corals close to the shore on *Kata Beach* and in the bay of *Ao Sane*. Better places for snorkelling are, for example, off *Ko He* (Coral Island) and *Ko Raya Yai*, and of course all around *Ko Phi Phi* as well as around *Ko Similan*, which is not only a top diving destination, the snorkelling is excellent too.

TRAVEL WITH KIDS

The chances of children finding friends to play with are higher on Phuket than anywhere else in Thailand, as many families come here for a holiday.

Phuket's beaches are one huge sandpit for children. However, some are more suitable than others. The central part of crowded Patong Beach is simply too crammed with loungers and sunshades. It is better to head for the less frequented northern and southern sections. Things are much quieter on the beaches of Bang Tao, Mai Khao, Nai Harn, Kata, Kata Noi and Karon. The bay of Ao Sane is not a suitable beach for children to swim, as corals and sharp-edged rocks can cause injury.

If your children get bored of beach life, you can take them to play a round of mini-golf with dinosaurs. It is worth noting that Thailand is one of the world's leading producers of children's clothing, which is extremely cheap in comparison to Europe or North America.

THE WEST COAST

ADVENTURE MINIGOLF
(118 B3) (*M C7*)

Phuket's mini-golf course, with 18 holes, is near *Bang Tao Beach* on the main road in the north of the tourist village. *Daily 11am–11pm | admission from 280 baht, children 200 baht | tel. 076 31 43 45 | www.phuketadventureminigolf. com*

Mini golf with dinosaurs, canoe tours and a climbing park in the jungle – Phuket is holiday heaven for the whole family

DINO PARK, KARON BEACH ⭐
(120 A4) (*📖 C11*)

Huge dinosaurs open their gaping, tooth-filled jaws, and after dark a fire-spitting volcano rumbles into action. All artificial, of course. This primeval land of fantasy is actually a crazy-golf course – fun for adults too! *Daily 10am–midnight | admission 240 baht, children 180 baht | Karon Rd. | on the hill between Kata and Karon Beach near the Marina Cottage resort | tel. 076 33 06 25 | www.dinopark. com*

INSIDER TIP QUEST LAGUNA ADVENTURE (118 B2) (*📖 C7*)

An adventure playground with jungle terrain awaits visitors with a good head for heights at Bang Tao Beach. This place is often used by companies for training sessions, but in the *family fun zone* kids from the age of six can learn to climb or (with ropes) clamber around the treetops. A whole afternoon of fun for kids costs only from 200 baht. *Laguna Beach Resort | Bang Tao Beach | tel. 076 31 42 53 | dev. lagunaphuket.com*

ROLLERBALL ZORBING
(120 B2) (*C10*)
Some things are just so crazy they must be great fun. This includes thundering down a 200 m/650 ft hill track inside an inflatable plastic ball filled with 40 l of water. Ever thought what it is like to be inside a washing machine.....? *Daily 10am–8pm | One ride 950 baht, six rides 1950 baht, free under 5 | Kalim Bay View, Soi 7 | Kalim Beach | tel. 08 98 72 65 32 | www.zorbingthailand.com*

SPLASH JUNGLE, MAI KHAO BEACH
(116 B2) (*C2*)
There is no jungle at all in this aquapark, but the "splashes" bit is true. The park's main attractions are a long flume, a pool with a wave machine and a water carousel *(Super Bowl)*. In the 335 m/365 yd-long "Lazy River" adults and children can let the current carry them gently in rubber rings. *Daily 10am–6pm | admission 1495 baht, children 750 baht, under-fives free | West Sands Resort | Mai Khao Beach | tel. 076 37 21 11 | www.splashjunglewaterpark.com*

SOUTH AND EAST COAST

INSIDER TIP ▶ PHUKET RIDING CLUB, CHALONG (120 C4) (*D12*)
Children too can get into the saddle here and trot through the rubber plantations or down to Mittrapab Beach. A guide accompanies the group. *Daily 7am–6.30pm | 1000 baht per hour through the jungle, 1,500 baht for 1,5 hours to the beach | Viset Rd. | road to Rawai, approx. 1.5 km/1 mile south of the roundabout | Chalong | tel. 076 28 82 13 | www.phuketridingclub.com*

SIAM SAFARI, CHALONG
(120 C4) (*D12*)
This tour operator, which has received various awards, offers a number of activities that children enjoy too, such as Land Rover trips or canoe tours. At the Siam Safari headquarters you can see how skilful monkeys are at picking coconuts. *Headquarters daily 9am–5pm | 45 Chao Fa Rd. | bypass from the airport, north of the roundabout | Chalong | tel. 076 28 01 16 | www.siamsafari.com*

SOI DOG'S PHUKET SHELTER ⊙
(116 B3) (*D3*)
The dogs' home run by this organisation is financed entirely by donations. It looks after Phuket's stray dogs and cats and also welcomes visitors. More than 400 animals have found a home here. North of the airport at Mai Khao Beach. For exact directions about how to get there, see the website. *Mon–Fri 9am–noon and 1–3.30pm, guided tours Mon–Fri 9.30am, 11am and 1.30pm | 167/9 Moo 4 | Soi Mai Khao 10 | www.soidog.org*

PHUKET TOWN & AROUND

BAAN TEELANKA (119 D5) (*E9*)
Your children will not believe their eyes when they see this house standing on its head. You enter it through the hole in the roof and then "walk up" to the living room where the furniture is hanging from the ceiling above your head. This upside-down world offers great photo opportunities. Try and visit during the week if you can because it gets extremely busy at weekends. *Daily 10am–6pm | admission 350 baht, children 4–11 years 190 baht | bypass Rd. towards the airport, near Siam Niramit | tel. 076 37 62 45 | upsidedownhouse-phuket.com*

PHUKET AQUARIUM (119 F6) (*ⅢF13*)

Children will be amazed at the diversity of fish swimming in the waters around Phuket. Fish in all shapes and sizes, from the beautiful to the downright bizarre, can be seen up close in this aquarium. The aquarium is also the nearest the children will get to manta rays, sharks, spiny lobsters and sea turtles on display in the 30 basins. Walking through the underwater tunnel is a particular highlight for young and old alike. *Daily 8.30am–4pm | admission 180 baht, children from a height of 100 cm 100 baht | south ofPhuket Town on Cape Phan Wa, signposted from there | www. phuketaquarium.org*

SIAM NIRAMIT ★ (119 D5) (*ⅢE9*)

In a theatre seating 1750, Niramit stages a gigantic show of culture and folklore *(Wed–Mon from 8.30pm)* with colourful costumes and great light effects. A village including a floating market was built on the site. At *Thai Village (from 5.30pm)* you and your children gain an impression of rural life in the four regions of Thailand. The demonstrations include the production of silk and making children's toys from grass. *Admission to show and village from 1500 baht, including buffet dinner from 1850 baht, children 1650 baht | pickup service by minibus from your hotel 300 baht per person (return) | northwest of Phuket Town on the bypass road to the airport, 3 km/2 miles north of the big Tesco Lotus supermarket | tel. 076 33 50 00 | www.siamniramit.com*

Playing, running around, splashing and swimming: Phuket has lots of child-friendly beaches

FESTIVALS & EVENTS

Many religious festivals and tourist events have different dates each year. For an up-to-date calendar of events, refer to the tourist office and the websites named here. The local Phuket Gazette also publishes information about events and celebrations, and has listings in the online edition *www.phuket gazette.net* (click on Events Calendar).

FESTIVALS & EVENTS

JANUARY/FEBRUARY

Phuket Old Town Festival: Fair in the old quarter. Music and shows take spectators back in the history of the island capital, which was greatly influenced by the Chinese. INSIDER TIP *Chinese New Year:* week-long *temple festival* at Wat Chalong on the bypass, road no. 4022, between Phuket Town and Rawai Beach. Fair, beauty contest, fireworks

APRIL

Songkran: No other Thai festival is celebrated as joyously as New Year. Battles on the water are held. At the beach of Nai Yang, sea turtles are released from the Laem Phan Wa breeding station.

Phuket Bike Week: Motorbike fans tour the island. Parties and events on Patong Beach. For the dates, see *www.phuketbikeweek.com*

Gay Pride Festival: Gay pride parade on Patong Beach. Dates at *www.phuket-pride.org*

MAY/JUNE & OCTOBER/NOVEMBER

INSIDER TIP *Loi Rüa:* Festival of the *Chao Leh* (sea gypsies) on Rawai Beach at the beginning and end of the monsoon season. Bamboo rafts supposedly carry all misfortune – in the shape of replica weapons and cut-off hair – out to sea.

JUNE

Phuket Marathon: In early June, you can watch (or participate in) the marathon, half marathon, walking (5 km/3.2miles) and children's run (2 km/1.2mile).
www.phuketmarathon.com

SEPTEMBER/OCTOBER

★ ● *Vegetarian Festival:* In honour of nine divine kings, who according to a legend ruled in China for 45,600 years. Chinese Thais eat vegetarian food for

nine days, enter a trance and flagellate themselves in processions through Phuket Town: they walk over red-hot coas and stick spikes and hooks through their cheeks and tongue. Visitors should wear white clothing. *www.phuketvegetarian.com*

NOVEMBER

Loi Kratong: The most romantic festival in Thailand. At full moon, boats are placed in the water with a candle, joss sticks, coins and flowers – on rivers, lakes and canals, on Phuket on swimming pools too. With the vanishing little boats, anger and frustration are supposed to float away and thus the soul can be cleansed.

DECEMBER

King's Cup Regatta: Yachts from all over the world compete by sailing off the southern tip of Phuket in early December. *www.kingscup.com*

Patong Carnival: Shows, live concerts, fireworks and a parade – celebrations for the start of the high season for tourism lasting several days.

NATIONAL HOLIDAYS

1 Jan	New Year's Day
Full moon Feb	*Makha Pucha*
6 April	*Chakri Day*
12–14 April	*Songkran*
1 May	Labour Day
Full moon in May	*Visakha Pucha (Buddha's birth, enlightenment, death)*
Full moon July	*Asaha Pucha (Buddha's first sermon)*
1 day after Asaha Pucha	*Khaopansa (start of the Buddhist fasting period)*
28 July	King Maha Vajiralongkorn's birthday
12 Aug	Queen Sirikit's birthday
13 Oct	Day of the death of King Bhumibol
23 Oct	Day of the death of king Chulalongkorn
5 Dec	Father's Day
10 Dec	Constitution Day
31 Dec	New Year's Eve

LINKS, BLOGS, APPS & MORE

LINKS & BLOGS

www.phuket.com Hotels, restaurants, nightlife, shopping, tours, beaches ... more or less every subject that could interest visitors to the island can be found here

www.phuketemagazine.com For beaches and restaurants, lifestyle and shopping – this online magazine operated by the Phuket tourist office presents the island, and has a lot of beautiful photos

www.phuket.net Useful tips not only for holidaymakers, but for those planning to stay longer thanks to a section on "living on Phuket"

www.faqs.org/faqs/thai/culture/ The history and culture of Thailand, Buddhism, Thai cuisine – not a colourful or hip website, but lots of solid information about the country and its people

www.travelfish.org Specialised in low-budget accommodation. This site states plainly what is good and bad, and is the coolest address on the web if you are looking for low-cost accommodation

www.jamiesphuketblog.com Jamie explores the island, getting off the beaten track, and presents almost everything that you can see and do on Phuket in his blog

www.phuket101.net Where can I get grilled insects? Where are the finest historic townhouses – and the wildest parties? The answers to these and other questions, as well as cool photos, can be found on this site

www.timinphuket.blogspot.de Tim takes you along with him to the markets and the beach, to restaurants, temples and everywhere else he goes on Phuket

www.phuketdining.com This is not just a website about eating out on Phuket. It also has information on many other subjects, and a collec-

Regardless of whether you are still researching your trip or already in Phuket: these addresses will provide you with more information, videos and networks to make your holiday even more enjoyable.

tion of videos about diving, cookery courses, restaurants, nightlife and many other themes

en.wikipedia.org/wiki/List_of_films_shot_in_Thailand If you want to travel in the footsteps of James Bond, Leonardo DiCaprio and others

www.phuketweather.net Not actually a weather site, but a list of all the webcams on Phuket, especially on the beaches. Also flight arrivals and departures on Phuket Airport

www.wheressharon.com/asia-with-kids/things-to-do-in-phuket-with-kids Personal recommendations (with pictures)of what to do in Phuket with kids

www.phuketbesttv.com Fashion shows, parties and rock concerts – whenever there is something happening, Phuket Best TV is there to film it

www.phuketgazette.net/tv Phuket's main English-language newspaper uploads videos

www.youtube.com/watch?v=9D6xZNbOcbM There's a beach on Phuket where you can do some serious planespotting – see for yourself!

www.youtube.com/watch?v=h7U6mm7UJBA Some impressions of the exotic street food on sale on the night market in Patong

Ultimate Phuket Guide This iPhone app guides you to hotspots dotted all over the island and includes GPS-based navigation. A concierge service is also available to organise services and tours

Phuketcity An app for iPhone and Android, specialised in hotel bookings

Phuket Island – GPS Map Navigator Wherever you may be on Phuket – the navigator on your iPhone willl find you and give you directions

Phuket City Guide The state tourism board app with a practical guide and augmented reality experience

TRAVEL TIPS

ACCOMMODATION

In the peak season from about 15 December to 10 January, many resorts charge supplements of 10 to 20 per cent. At many resorts guests must pay a steep price for compulsory dinner at Christmas and New Year. Check this in advance if you book a hotel at this time of the year. In the off-peak season (April to October) price reductions of up to 40 per cent are possible. You can sometimes save a lot of money by booking via internet, directly or through a hotel reservation service such as *www.phuket-hotels.com* and *www.asiarooms.com*. Booking a package holiday can be cheaper than making your own arrangements.

ARRIVAL

✈ Many operators of charter flights *(see www.phuketairportonline. com)* go to Phuket directly from Europe.

RESPONSIBLE TRAVEL

It doesn't take a lot to be environmentally friendly whilst travelling. Don't just think about your carbon footprint whilst flying to and from your holiday destination but also about how you can protect nature and culture abroad. As a tourist it is especially important to respect nature, look out for local products, cycle instead of driving, save water and much more. If you would like to find out more about eco-tourism please visit: *www.ecotourism.org*

You'll find cheap flights at *www.flight-centre.co.uk; www.cheapticket.co.uk; www.cheapflights.co.uk; www.travel supermarket.com; www.southalltravel. co.uk* and many other internet agencies, but it's also worth contacting airlines such as Qatar Airways direct. Bangkok's international Suvarnabhumi airport (pronounced: *Suwannapum | www.airportsu varnabhumi.com*) is a hub for Southeast Asia and served by most European and Asian airlines. Flight time from London is approx. 11 hours. Even during the December/January high season, non-stop return flights from London to Bangkok with major airlines such British Airways or Thai Airways are available for around £900 (US-$ 1400); cheap return flights to Bangkok or Phuket with one stopover can be had for as little as £400 (US-$ 630). From Suvarnabhumi, Thai Airways and Bangkok Airways *(www.bangkokair. com)* fly to Phuket several times daily. You can normally expect to pay between 50 and 80 euros one way. Budget airline Air Asia *(www.airasia.com)* flies to Phuket from the old airport, Don Muang. A further budget airline, Nok Air *(www. nokair.com),* operates a service from Dong Muang. The flight from there to Phuket costs approx. 1,300 baht.

From the airport in Phuket, the bus to the terminal in Phuket Town costs 100 baht. The limousine service will take you to all beaches for a fixed amount but costs twice as much as a public taxi. To find the taxi rank, go right when you leave the arrivals concourse. Before setting off make sure that the driver is willing to switch on the meter – they do not always want to do so, especially during rush hour.

From arrival to weather

BANKS & CREDIT CARDS

At banks you can change travellers' cheques denominated in dollars and other currencies *(Mon–Fri 8.30am–3.30pm, bureaux de change daily, often until 10pm)*. If you pay by credit card, many shops increase the price. You can also get cash with your credit card by showing a passport, but this is usually easier at a cashpoint (ATM). Visa and MasterCard are accepted by all banks. At many cashpoints bearing the Maestro sign you can get cash using your normal bank card. Branches of Bangkok Bank also accept American Express. A fee of 150 baht is charged per cash withdrawal. If you lose your card, do not fail to inform your bank immediately.

BEACHES

Phuket's beaches are among the best and the easiest to reach in the whole of Thailand. The majority can be accessed by car and offer all the amenities such as accommodation, restaurants, diving centres, bars and shops.

CAR HIRE

A rental car is a good way of exploring the island (Jeeps for about approx. 1000 baht, air-conditioned cars approx. 1600 baht per day, reductions for longer hire periods). Hire desks for Avis *(tel. 076 35 12 43 | www.avisthailand.com)* and Budget *(tel. 076 20 53 96 | www.budget.co.th)* are situated at the airport and in large hotels. *Pure Car Rent (Phuket Town | 75 Rasada Rd. | tel. 076 21 10 02 | www.purecarrent.com)* has a

BUDGETING

Beer	£ 1.45 / $ 1.85	*for 0.3 litres in a bar*
Scarf	from £ 5.35 / $ 7	*for a batik scarf*
Massage	approx. £ 7 / $ 9.30	*on the beach*
Soup	£ 0.80 / $ 1.20	*for noodle soup at a food stall*
Petrol	£ 0.80 / $ 1.20	*for 1 litre premium fuel*
Fruit	£ 0.20 / $ 0.30	*for a whole fruit*

good reputation. Traffic drives on the left. An international driving licence is required. Ensure you have insurance that includes damage to persons as well as to property. Reputable agencies have the appropriate policies. Avoid car-hire agencies at the roadside which offer private cars or other vehicles which are not registered as hire cars. What might look like a bargain could turn out to be very expensive. A hire-car with driver is worth considering as an alternative to driving yourself *(adding approx. 500 baht to the cost, for 8 hours)*.

CHILD PROTECTION

At night children go from bar to bar, selling cigarettes, chewing gum and flowers, especially on Patong Beach. The child protection organisation *Childwatch Phuket (www.childwatchphuket.org)* states: "The more they sell, the more certain it is that they will have to work into the early hours. However appealing their eyes, and however much sympathy you feel for them, it is better for the children if you buy nothing."

CLIMATE, WHEN TO GO

In the period from November to February the weather is what many Europeans and North Americans regard as an ideal summer. After that, and until May, it gets very hot and does not cool off much at night. In the rainy season (May to October/November) temperatures fall a little. Most rain falls between mid-August and mid-October. A good weather website is *www.phuket-weather.blogspot.com.*

CONSULATES & EMBASSIES

UK EMBASSY
14 Wireless Road | Lumpini, Pathumwan | Bangkok 10330 | tel. 0 23 05 83 33 | www.ukinthailand.fco.gov.uk | Mon–Thu 8am–noon and 12:45pm–4:30pm; Fri 8am–1 pm

US EMBASSY
American Citizen Services | U.S. Embassy | 95 Wireless Road | Bangkok 10330 | tel. 0 22 05 40 00 | th.usembassy.gov | Mon–Fri 7:30–11am and 1–2pm

UK HONORARY CONSULATE
If you require consular assistance in Phuket, please call the British Embassy in Bangkok on 02 305 8333 and follow the instructions to speak to a member of consular staff.

CUSTOMS

Cash amounting to more than 10,000 US dollars must be declared on arrival in Thailand. It is forbidden to export statues of Buddha. Export of antiques and animal products requires a permit. Travellers returning to the European Union have the following duty-free allowance: 200 cigarettes, 250 g of tobacco or 50 cigars, 2 litres of wine and 1 litre of spirits, 500 g of coffee, 50 g of perfume, 250 ml of eau de toilette and other goods to a value of £ 390/560 US dollars (when flying). When entering the USA, goods to a value of $ 800 including 2 litres of alcoholic drinks are duty-free (see *www.cbp.gov* for all details).

ELECTRICITY

220-volt power supply. Adapters are sold in electric goods shops.

HEALTH

No vaccinations are necessary before visiting Phuket. There is no risk of contracting malaria on the island, however it is still recommended to consult your doctor regarding vaccinations before your holiday as there is a real threat of dengue fever. It is therefore important to use the necessary mosquito repellent and nets (the yellow fever mosquito is daytime active).

It is not advisable to drink tap water. However, you need not have reservations about eating street food, even from basic stalls, as Thais are careful about preparing snacks and meals.

Medical care on Phuket is excellent. The best hospital on the island is the *Bangkok Phuket Hospital (tel. 076 25 44 25 | www.phukethospital.com)*, and the *Phuket International Hospital (tel. 076 24 94 00 | www.phuketinternational hospital.com)* also meets international standards. English-speaking staff are present at both. Contact the hospitals to get an ambulance. The dentists on the island also have high standards at prices much lower than in Europe and the USA.

IMMIGRATION

For a visit not exceeding 30 days, visitors from many countries, including the UK, do not need a visa to enter Thailand, just a passport valid for at least 6 months, and a return or onward ticket. If you plan to stay more than a month, obtain a 60-day visa at a Thai consulate or embassy in your country before leaving home. Check www.thaivisa.com or the websites of Thailand's immigration authority (www.immigration.go.th) and the Ministry of Foreign Affairs (www.mfa.go.th) for details. Those who overstay are forced to pay a fine of 500 baht a day when they leave.

DIPLOMATIC REPRESENTATION
UK: *Royal Thai Embassy in London | 29–30 Queen's Gate | London SW7 5JB | tel. 030 79 48 10 | www.thaiembassyuk. org.uk*
US: *Royal Thai Embassy in Washington | 1024 Wisconsin Ave. | N.W. Washington D.C. 20007 | tel. 202 9 44 36 00 | www. thaiembdc.org*

INFORMATION

THAILAND TOURIST AUTHORITY (TAT)
UK: *17–19 Cockspur Street | London SW1Y 5BL | tel. 0870 900 2007 | www. tourismthailand.org*
US: *Broadway, Suite 2810 | New York, NY 10006 | tel. 212/432-0433 | www. tourismthailand.org*
Australia: *Level 20, 56 Pit Street | Sydney, NSW 2000 | tel. (02) 9247 7549 | www.tourismthailand.org*

TOURISM AUTHORITY OF THAILAND (TAT)
Information desk at the airport. *191 Thalang Rd. | tel. 076 21 10 36, tel. 076 21 22 13 |*

INTERNET & WIFI

Nearly every resort and many restaurants offer free Wi-Fi hotspots. That said, some of the exclusive resorts charge guests exorbitant prices for this service. You should therefore inquire about the Wi-Fi charges before using it. It costs just a few baht per minute to go online with a modem and a Thai Internet SIM card. Many shops and 7-Eleven minima-

CURRENCY CONVERTER

£	THB	THB	£
1	43.55	10	0.23
3	131	30	0.69
5	218	50	1.15
13	566	130	2.99
40	1,742	400	9.19
75	3,266	750	17.23
120	5,225	1,200	27.57
250	10,886	2,500	57.44
500	21,764	5,000	114.88

$	THB	THB	$
1	33.32	10	0.30
3	100	30	0.90
5	167	50	1.50
13	433	130	3.90
40	1,332	400	12
75	2,498	750	22.52
120	3,996	1,200	36.03
250	8,326	2,500	75.06
500	16,652	5,000	150.13

For current exchange rates see www.xe.com

rkets sell SIM cards (you need to show your passport).

PHONE & MOBILE PHONE

The country code for the UK is 0044, for the USA and Canada 001, for Ireland 00353. Then dial the town or area code without a zero. The code for phoning Phuket from abroad is 006676.

Phone cards for public telephones are available from post/telecommunications offices and many shops. The better hotels have IDD phones in the rooms, enabling guests to make international calls direct, usually at high rates. Phoning with your mobile phone usually incurs roaming charges, and you bear part of the costs of incoming calls. To avoid this, you can replace your SIM card from home with a Thai SIM card. Pre-paid cards are on sale everywhere. Thai providers of mobile telephony often offer particular country codes at special rates. True Move, for example, offers calls to Europe via internet from 1 baht per minute. On average a minute to Europe using a special code costs 8 baht. The three main providers are AIS *(www.ais.co.th/12call/en/index. html)*, DTAC *(www.happy.co.th/home_ en.php)* and True Move *(www.true moveh.truecorp.co.th)*. In many shops you can get a low-price second mobile phone for using a Thai SIM card. Basic mobile phones are sold for approx. 20 euros, second-hand ones for even less.

WEATHER IN PHUKET

	Jan	Feb	March	April	May	June	July	Aug	Sept	Oct	Nov	Dec
Daytime temperatures in °C/ °F	31/88	32/90	33/91	33/91	31/88	31/88	30/86	30/86	30/86	30/86	30/86	31/88
Nighttime temperatures in °C/ °F	22/72	22/72	23/73	24/75	24/75	25/77	24/75	25/77	24/75	24/75	23/73	22/72
☀ Sunshine hours/day	9	9	8	8	7	6	6	6	6	5	5	7
☂ Precipitation days/month	4	4	7	15	20	19	17	18	20	20	15	8
≈ Water temperatures in °C/ °F	27/81	28/82	29/84	29/84	29/84	28/82	28/82	28/82	28/82	28/82	28/82	27/81

☀ Sunshine hours/day ☂ Precipitation days/month ≈ Water temperatures in °C/ °F

POST

Airmail to Europe and North America up to 10 g costs 17 baht, postcards 15 baht. It normally takes 5 to 7 days for letters and cards to arrive. Air-mail parcels (5 kg) cost about 2500 baht. The main post office is in Phuket Town *(Montri Rd. | Mon–Fri 8.30am–4.30pm, Sat 9am–noon)*.

PRICES & ADMISSION FEES

A meal with rice at a basic eatery costs no more than 60 baht. A two-course menu seldom costs more than 250 baht. Prices are fixed in supermarkets and big shopping centres. Elsewhere you bargain. Thais do not regard it as unfair to charge foreigners more. A two-price system is perfectly usual in many privately run establishments such as zoos and fun parks. State institutions such as national parks and museums also have higher admission prices for foreigners.

PUBLIC TRANSPORT

There is one major drawback to public transport: buses and covered pick-ups with bench seating are cheap, but they only run between 7am and approx. 5pm – and then only from the beaches to Phuket Town *(to Ranong Rd., near the roundabout)*. If you want to go from one beach to another without a detour via the town, or to travel in the evening, you have to hire a tuk tuk – and bargain!

TAXI

Taxis installed with taximeters can only be found at the airport. At the beaches, you will find a whole host of smaller operators who offer trips at fixed rates, which can be extremely steep. The island's buses are a cheaper alternative which offer a shuttle service between Phuket Town and the beaches from 6am to 4pm.

TIME

Thailand time is GMT plus 7 hours throughout the year (New York plus 14 hours, Australia minus 3 hours).

TIPPING

In many better restaurants there is a *service charge* of ten per cent. You should then pay a tip only if the service was especially good. Ten per cent is a suitable tip in restaurants without a service charge. Taxi drivers do not normally get a tip.

TOURIST POLICE

Nationwide emergency hotline: *tel. 1155.* Station in Phuket Town: *100/31-32, Chalermphakeat Rd. (Bypass Rd. towards the airport, opposite Gems Gallery) | phuketdir.com/pkttouristpolice*

TRANSCRIPTION

There is no generally applicable system of transcribing Thai words and names in the Roman alphabet, which means you see various spellings of some words.

ROAD ATLAS

The green line indicates the Discovery Tour "Phuket at a glance"
The blue line indicates the other Discovery Tours

All tours are also marked on the pull-out map

Photo: Ko Phi Phi

Exploring Phuket

The map on the back cover shows how the area has been sub-divided

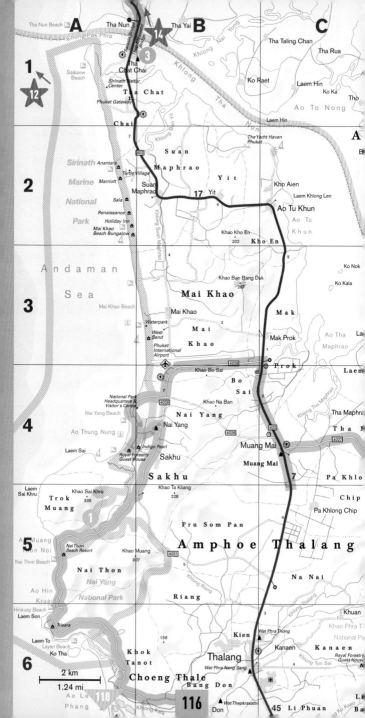

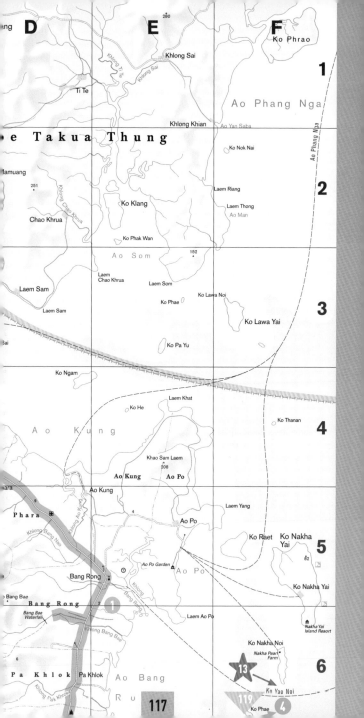

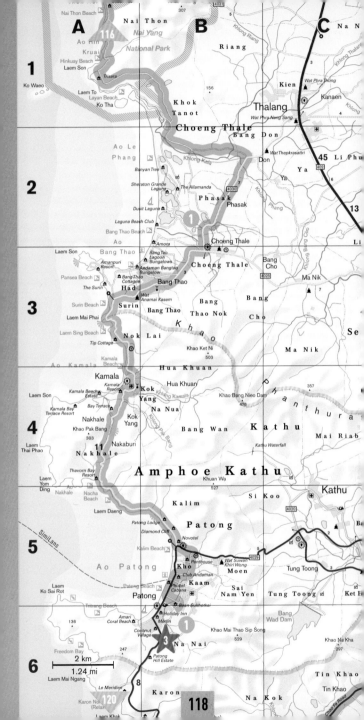

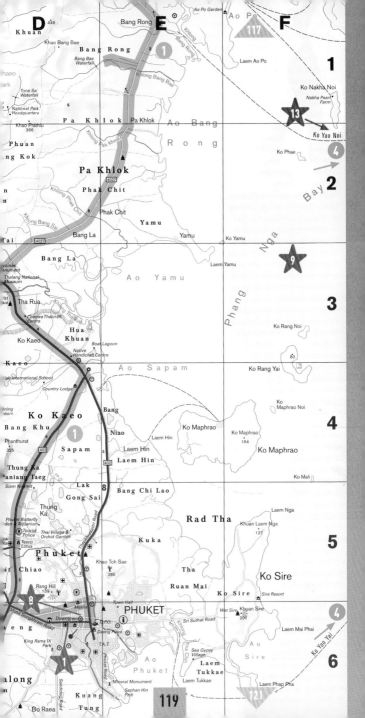

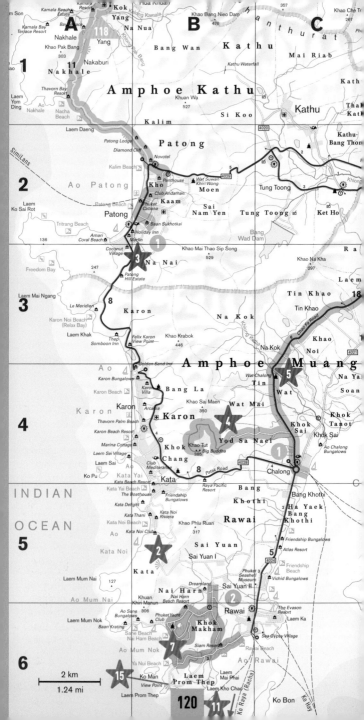

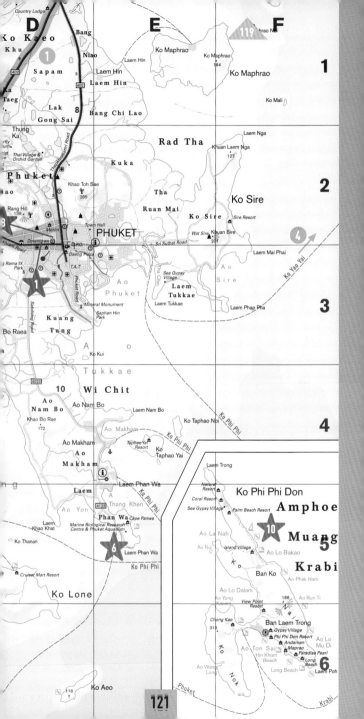

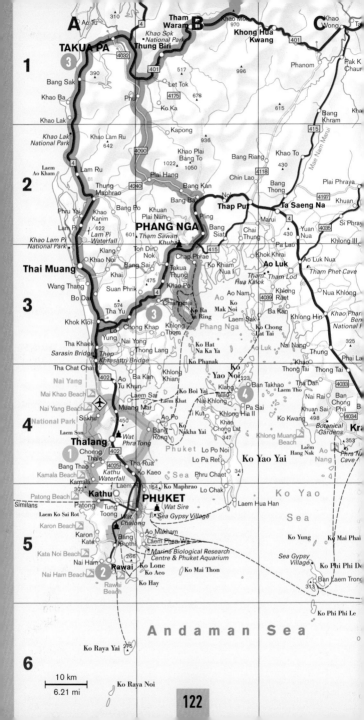

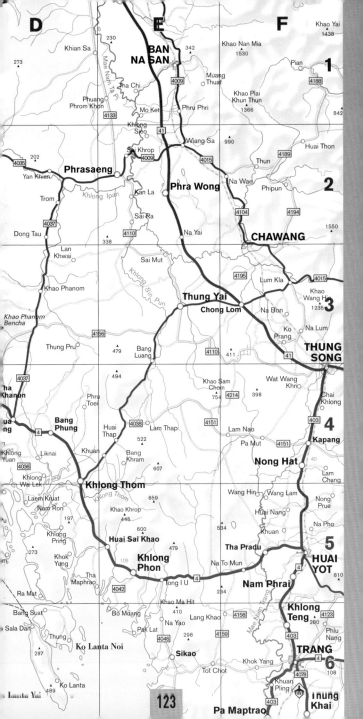

KEY TO ROAD ATLAS

Highway Fernverkehrsstraße Grande route de transit Strada di transito	Hospital Krankenhaus Hôpital Ospedale
Main road Hauptstraße Route principale Strada principale	Police Polizei Police Polizia
Secondary road Nebenstraße Route secondaire Strada secondaria	Broadcasting station Funkstation Station radio Stazione radio
Carriage way, Path Fahrweg, Pfad Chemin carrosable, Sentier Strada carrozzabile, Sentiero	Waterfall Wasserfall Cascade Cascata
Petrol station Tankstelle Station essence Stazione di rifornimento	Golf Golf Golf Golf
Distance in km Entfernung in km Distance en km Distanze in km	Harbour Hafen Port Porto
County boundary Bezirksgrenze Frontière de province Confine di provincia	Point of interest Sehenswürdigkeit Curiosité Curiosità
Parish boundary Gemeindegrenze Front. de commune Conf. di municipio	Hotel Hotel Hôtel Albergo
Airport Flughafen Aéroport Aeroporto	Beach Strand Plage Spiaggia
Information Information Informations Informazione	Scuba diving Sporttauchen Sous-marine plongée Sport subaqueo
Buddhist temple Buddha-Tempel Temple bouddhique Tempio buddista	Waterskiing Wasserski Ski nautique Sci nautico
Chinese temple Chinesischer Tempel Temple chinois Tempio cinese	Yachting Segelsport Centre de voile Sport velico
Mosque Moschee Mosquée Moschea	View point Aussichtspunkt Vue panoramique Panorama
Church Kirche Église Chiesa	National park Nationalpark Parc national Parco nazionale
Monument Denkmal Monument Monumento	MARCO POLO Discovery Tour 1 MARCO POLO Erlebnistour 1 MARCO POLO Tour d'aventure 1 MARCO POLO Giro aventura 1
Post office Postamt Poste Posta	MARCO POLO Discovery Tours MARCO POLO Erlebnistouren MARCO POLO Tours d'aventure MARCO POLO Giri awenturosi
MARCO POLO Highlight	

INDEX

This index lists all sights, islands (Ko), beaches and bays, destinations for trips and important persons or themes mentioned in the guide. Page numbers in bold refer to the main entry.

WRITE TO US

e-mail: info@marcopologuides.co.uk

Did you have a great holiday?
Is there something on your mind?
Whatever it is, let us know!
Whether you want to praise, alert us
to errors or give us a personal tip –
MARCO POLO would be pleased to
hear from you.
We do everything we can to provide the
very latest information for your trip.

Nevertheless, despite all of our authors'
thorough research, errors can creep in.
MARCO POLO does not accept any
liability for this. Please contact us by
e-mail or post.

MARCO POLO Travel Publishing Ltd
Pinewood, Chineham Business Park
Crockford Lane, Chineham
Basingstoke, Hampshire RG24 8AL
United Kingdom

PICTURE CREDITS
Cover Photograph: Longtail boats on Paradise Beach (Look/Design Pics)
Images: DuMont Bildarchiv: Sasse (78, 107); W. Hahn (8, 60); huber-images: Schmid (flap right, 12/13), M. Shippen (47), Stadler (28 right), L. Vaccarella (40); Laif: Amme (38), Heuer (11, 45), Sasse (flap left, 34, 55); Laif/Polaris: C. Brown (19 bottom); Laif/Redux: B. Lewin (19 top); Look/Design Pics (1); Mai Khao Marine Turtle Foundation: Ornjaree Nawee (18 bottom); mauritius images: J. Warburton-Lee (82); mauritius images/Alamy (3, 7, 10, 20/21, 30, 30/31, 32/33, 56, 64, 66/67, 68, 81, 84/85, 87, 89, 92), M. Azavedo (18 top), P. Treanor (50), N. Uttamaharad (4 bottom, 63); mauritius images/Alamy/AA World Travel Library (42); mauritius images/Alamy/Realy Easy Star: L. Cervetto (53); mauritius images/ib: Kreder (6), Stella (103); mauritius images/Imagebroker: J. Beck (37), M. Moxter (74/75, 100/101, 118/119), N. Probst (58/59); mauritius images/Mito images: P. Kunkel (18 centre); mauritius images/Pacific Stock (2); mauritius images/Prisma (99); H. Mielke (14/15, 31, 96/97); O. Stadler (4 top, 26/27, 76/77); O. Stadler/A. Stubhan (5, 17, 22, 24, 28 left, 29, 49, 71, 72, 104, 106 top, 106 bottom); M. Weigt (9, 104/105)

2nd Edition 2019
Worldwide Distribution: Marco Polo Travel Publishing Ltd, Pinewood, Chineham Business Park,
Crockford Lane, Basingstoke, Hampshire RG24 8AL, United Kingdom. E-mail: sales@marcopolouk.com
© MAIRDUMONT GmbH & Co. KG, Ostfildern
Chief editor: Marion Zorn
Author: Wilfried Hahn, co-author: Mark Markand; editor: Karin Liebe
Programme supervision: Lucas Forst-Gill, Susanne Heimburger, Tamara Hub, Johanna Jiranek, Nikolai Michaelis,
Kristin Wittemann, Tim Wohlbold
Picture editor: Gabriele Forst; What's hot: Mark Markand, wunder media, Munich; Cartography road atlas &
pull-out map: © MAIRDUMONT, Ostfildern; Design front cover, p. 1, pull-out map cover: Karl Anders – Büro für
Visual Stories, Hamburg; interior: milchhof:atelier, Berlin; Discovery Tours, p. 2/3: Susan Chaaban Dipl.-Des. (FH)
Translated from German by Susan Jones; Prepress: writehouse, Cologne

MIX
Paper from
responsible sources
FSC
www.fsc.org
FSC® C124385

DOS & DON'TS 👆

Here are a few things to look out for on your Phuket holiday

DON'T UNDERESTIMATE THE SUN

A lot of tourists sit on deck on the ferries to the islands. The wind cools their faces, they don't notice that the sun is shining as intensely as on the beach – and arrive with severe sunburn. Use sun-blocker, and better still shield your skin from the sun altogether on ferries.

DON'T DRIVE A MOTORBIKE WITHOUT A HELMET

Motorcyclists and their passengers are obliged to wear helmets. You can often see three or four locals on a motorbike without helmets, but tourists should not emulate them, as it is no use pointing out what the locals do if you are stopped at one of the frequent police checks. On average there is one fatal accident every day, and tourists are regularly among the casualties. Note also that the only third-party insurance available for using a motorbike covers injuries to others only up to a sum of 15,000 baht.

DON'T ARGUE WITH THAIS

Generally speaking, Thais are not argumentative and show international tourists a great deal of respect. However, even the calmest of folk can lose their patience once in a while, especially if a Thai person thinks he has 'lost his face' (without the foreigner really understanding why). If you see a situation escalating, the best thing to do is back down with an apologetic smile.

DON'T GET CARRIED AWAY WITH A WATER SCOOTER

You can zip over the waves on a water scooter, but it might be an annoyance to others and even cause serious injuries. On Phuket they are only allowed on the beaches of Bang Tao, Karon, Kata and Patong. If you zoom off to another beach, you can be fined.

DON'T FEEL TOO SECURE

Southern Thailand is a safe place to travel on the whole, but do pay attention to a few guidelines about staying safe. Women should not walk on lonely beaches or hitchhike unaccompanied. Be on your guard in the tourist areas of Phuket on little-used roads at night – foreigners riding mopeds have been attacked and robbed. Flashing a well-filled wallet around in a bar can arouse desires. If invited to join locals for a drinking session, say no politely or leave after having one drink, as pent-up frustrations can be explosive when Thais get drunk.

DON'T IGNORE RED FLAGS

From early May until November or December dangerous rip currents often occur on Phuket's beaches. There are fatalities every year because holidaymakers ignore the red flags and enter the water.